D1717091

Wake Up Black People: Are Our Communities in Peril? (Dreams Do Come True!)

The Status Of African American Communities, Past, and Present!

by

DE VERE O. KELLEY

Dorrance Publishing Co
585 Alpha Drive
Pittsburgh, PA 15238
Visit our website at *www.dorrancebookstore.com*

ISBN: 978-1-6386-7251-7
eISBN: 978-1-6386-7603-4

Gary, Indiana

"The future
belongs to
those who
prepare for
it today."

Malcolm X

Life is a dance and it is your dreams that takes the lead.
Life is such a challenge and you have
to be willing to pursue your goals.

Don't allow the world to determine what your contributions will be
in society as you pursue your place in this world.

Pursue your ambitions with many expectations
that you have set for yourself.

Strive forth with perseverance for the things
that are important to you and your destiny.

Please don't accept handouts from anyone.

Everything that you accomplish will be initiated by your efforts.

Make sure that you don't take
anything or anyone for granted.

Life is just too short to become complacent about anything!

DE VERE O. KELLEY

Dedication

"I have often asked myself how fascinating it was to have worked in education and public libraries for many decades. Throughout my long and successful career, I was blessed to have had the opportunity to work with such talented English teachers, media specialists, librarians, support staff, superintendents and administrators. The students that captured my heart were just phenomenal and they were the highlight of my career. It was the students that kept a smile on my face everyday throughout my career as a media specialist. I am so grateful for crossing paths with so many kind people throughout my career and for their confidence in my talent, skills and my dedication to my profession. It is a pleasure to dedicate my first manuscript to all of them. Enough said!!!!"

DE VERE KELLEY

"When Are WE Going to Get Over It?" By Andrew Michael Manis

For much of the last forty years, ever since America "fixed" its race problem in the Civil Rights and Voting Rights Acts, we white people have been impatient with African Americans who continued to blame race for their difficulties. Often we have heard whites ask, "When are African Americans finally going to get over it?" Now I want to ask: "When are we White Americans going to get over our ridiculous obsession with skin color?"

Recent reports that "Election Spurs Hundreds' of Race Threats, Crimes" should frighten and infuriate every one of us. Having grown up in "Bombingham," Alabama in the 1960s, I remember overhearing an avalanche of comments about what many white classmates and their parents wanted to do to John and Bobby Kennedy and Martin Luther King Jr. Eventually, as you may recall, in all three cases, someone decided to do more than "talk the talk."

Since our recent presidential term when Obama was the candidate, to our eternal shame we are once again hearing the same reprehensible talk that I remember from my boyhood. We, white people, have controlled political life in the disunited colonies and United States for some 400 years on this continent. Conservative whites have been in power for twenty-eight of the last forty years. Even during the eight Clinton years, conservatives in Congress blocked most of his agenda and pulled him to the right.

Yet never in that period did I read any headlines suggesting that anyone was calling for the assassinations of presidents Nixon, Ford, Reagan, or either of the Bushes. Criticize them, yes. Call for their impeachment, perhaps. But there were no bounties on their heads. And even when someone did try to kill Ronald Reagan, the perpetrator was a non-political mental case who wanted merely to impress Jody Foster.

But elect a liberal who happens to be Black and we're back in the sixties again. At this point in our history, we should be proud that we've proven what conservatives are always saying – that in America anything is possible, EVEN electing a black man as president. But instead, we now hear that school children from Maine to California are talking about wanting to "assassinate Obama."

Fighting the urge to throw up, I can only ask, "How Long?" How long before we white people realize we can't make our nation, much less the whole world, look like us? How long until we white people can – once and for all – get over this hell-conceived preoccupation with skin color? How long until we white people get over the demonic conviction that white skin makes us superior? How long before we white people get over our bitter resentments about being demoted to the status of equality with non-whites? How long before we get over our expectations that we should be at the head of the line merely because of our white skin? How long until we white people end our silence and call out peers when they share the latest jokes in the privacy of our white-only conversations?

I believe in free speech, but how long until we white people start making racist loudmouths as socially uncomfortable as we do flag burners? How long until we white people will stop insisting that blacks exercise personal responsibility, build strong families, educate themselves enough to edit the *Harvard Law Review*, and work hard enough to become President of the United States, only to threaten to assassinate them when they do?

How long before we start "living out the true meaning" of our creeds, both civil and religious, that all men and women are created equal and that "red and yellow, black and white" all are precious in God's sight?

Until November 4, 2008, I didn't believe this country would ever elect an African American to the presidency. I still don't believe I'll live long enough to see us white people get over our racism problem. But there's my three-point plan: First, every day that Barack Obama lives in the White House that Black Slaves Built, I am going to pray that God (all the Secret Service) will protect him and his family from us, white people. Second, I am going to report to the FBI any white person I overhear saying, in seriousness or jest, anything of a threatening nature about President Obama. Third, I'm going to pray to live long enough to see America surprise the world once again, when white people can "in spirit and truth" sing of our damnable color prejudice, "We HAVE overcome."

I have held on to this letter since it was written in 2004 when Barack Obama was running for president of the United States. What a provocative and inspiring piece of literature that was written by a distinguished professor in Macon, Georgia.

Who would have thought that a white professor could have expressed my feelings as a black man so vividly as a reflection of how many blacks have felt for decades? This letter strummed on my heartstrings because so many of the comments are accurate. I could have easily written this letter myself because it expresses so many of my views and I am sure other Blacks feel the same way. It was very evident that he has read and studied the history of African Americans by being very decisive in his views as he expresses the contents of this letter which are coming straight from his heart and by the things that he has examined over the years as Blacks continue to deal with racism. It has been one of the hardest stains to remove in the fabric of America and it will continue to be a stain very difficult to remove.

You have to wonder if other White Americans that would have read this letter years ago and taken Professor Andrew M. Manis's comments very seriously would we have less unrest in the world. This letter should have given some whites a different perspective. There might have been fewer police murders of black men, less rioting, fewer protests, and other evils that have been a part of our trajectory that seemed to surface during the 2020 Presidential Election. Blacks are all about protecting society with great police officers and black and white. We need to open our eyes and clear the fog and start looking at America in a manner that is going to continue to be beneficial for everyone as we continue to focus on eradicating some of the evils that have been detrimental to blacks in our society. When one person suffers, we all suffer. We also have to remember that "We All

Are God's Children." Humans created racism, God didn't and it is going to be left up to humans to change this trajectory with a strong determination by the majority of whites working in harmony with blacks.

Andrew Michael Manis is an associate professor of history at Macon State College and wrote this as an editorial in the *Macon Telegraph*. Posted September 26, 2009.

Contents

Chapter One 1

Perspective

Chapter Two 19

Factors That Have Contributed to the Hardships of Some Blacks

Marijuana 20

Marijuana – The Effects .21

Crack Cocaine 24

Systemic Racism 26

Systemic Poverty and Welfare 28

Black Wealth Inequality .33

Black Homicide in America (Past and Present) 39

Race Riots (1960 – Present) 44

Police Killing Blacks 47

Blacks Incarcerated 52

Protests and Demonstrations 56

The Impact of Looting 58

The Incarceration of Black Women 62

Factors That Have Contributed to Incarceration of Black Women 69

Chapter Three 75

Closing the Achievement Gap of Blacks in Education

The Burden of Poverty 80

The Challenges of School 83
Training for Teachers 85
Recommendations for Eliminating the Achievement Gap for African Americans 85
College Education Disparities of Blacks and Latinos 87

Chapter Four 95
True Stories of Bad Behavior and Bad Choices
Dwayne
Randall
Larry
Charlie
Katrina
William
Rosie and Richard
The Postman and His Wife (Gregory and Sandra)

Chapter Five 145
The Black Family

Chapter Six 157
The Art of Good Parenting

Chapter Seven 169
Nutrition and the African American Diet
Examining the Life Expectancy of Blacks 177

Chapter Eight 187
Black Voter Suppression (The 1800s – Present)
Black Stereotypes of the Past and Present 195

Chapter Nine 203
The Impact of the Coronavirus (2019 – Present)
COVID-19 Vaccines and People of Color 207

Chapter Ten 211
Law Enforcement (The Police) and Blacks

Chapter Eleven 219
The Law Enforcement (Police) Quiz

Chapter Twelve 233
Final Thoughts

The Key to Success Poem 231
The Resource Library 241
References Cited 255
Answers to the Law Enforcement (Police) Quiz 263
Glossary of Terms 265
Index 271
About the Author 273

Chapter One

Perspective

This book was not written to place blame and judgment on African Americans. It is just an analysis of the behavior that I have seen over the years dating back from the early 1950s to the present day. It wasn't written out of anger or maliciousness, but it was written by the analysis of things that I experienced growing up in a Midwestern town in Indiana. This book was written because I am still trying to figure out why some things occurred in my hometown of Gary. The neighborhoods have changed drastically. Some neighborhoods are still rundown in 2022 and almost dilapidated. My neighborhood was beautiful when I was growing up as a child. You have to drive cautiously through some of the neighborhoods in Gary because of the terrible condition of some of the streets. Growing up in urban Gary was a very delightful experience for me. In the late '50s and beyond, it was just vibrant, and your neighbors felt like your brothers and sisters. You didn't have the fear of people breaking into your home when you weren't home. If you drive through Gary today, you might get shot accidentally. Some decline of Gary started in the late '70s. Some neighborhoods started to deteriorate before the '70s. Things started to go downhill in the community. All the neighborhoods weren't on the decline. I did not find some areas recognizable after returning in the late 2000s. The house that I grew up in no longer exists. A narrative to follow as to what happened to my childhood residence. It was very disheartening to lose my childhood home. Illegal drug usage created some of the dynamics in my hometown growing up and people selling drugs, crime is still a major issue in Gary. You have to use caution driving around Gary today because of the peril. It can be a very frightening experience.

We can continue to be victims of a society and we can say that for some reason the world has been cold and unkind to us. We can't blame white people for all our peril. We have to ask ourselves, are we the cause of some of the problems, hardships, and other issues that have plagued African Americans for years? Why do we continue to sell and kill each other over drugs? Some things have been out of our control and some things could have been prevented by our conscience and integrity. The Coronavirus was out of our control and the impact that it had on our well-being was devastating. I have been asking myself for years, how did my people allow these terrible things to happen to them, drug usage, selling drugs, crime, homicides, etc.? I sat in the shadows for years watching things evolve in my community and at home that was beyond my comprehension as a child and teenager growing up in a predominantly black community. All black communities do not have these issues.

This narrative began in the early late fifties in a town with a population of about 175,415. Some of the names and locations in this book have been modified or changed for privacy. I lived in a neighborhood that I would say was decent and livable. We lived next door to a housing complex and the name of the complex was West Park Manor. When our home was built in the late fifties, there were not that many homes in the neighborhood. Development was just beginning to flourish. Everything seemed new to me as a child growing up in Gary. I can remember playing in construction zones when homes started turning up everywhere. I played with many friends in these construction zones. We had fun looking at the construction tractors and seeing the large holes dug to create roads.

West Park Manor (The Projects) was developed after the establishment of the neighborhood where I lived. There was an elementary school located across the street from where I lived in Gary. All the children in the neighborhood attended this elementary school so I knew just about everyone in the neighborhood. The children in this neighborhood would eventually end up at the middle school and the high school. In the early 1960s, the school district was predominantly white. When I graduated from Gary High School in 1977, the student body was 95 percent Black. Whites had drifted to other cities around Gary.

Our family was friends with the families that lived in the housing complex, West Park Manor. These homes were built to last with a concrete foundation, and they were very solid in structure. The complex was composed of about eighty buildings with three- and four-bedroom units. This complex was well-known and well-respected from the early 1970s until the decline in the late '80s. People took pride in the complex with well-manicured lawns and beautiful flowers that draped the buildings. The grass was always green, and people seemed to enjoy living in The Projects as they were called and referred to. These units are still standing but you wouldn't recognize some of the buildings because of their demise. The grass isn't maintained, and garbage cans are more visible as you drive through the complex. Gates have been constructed in certain locations to keep some people out looking like a gated prison. Crime has risen substantially in this complex and the neighborhood. This complex was renovated around 2000 but you would not know that by looking at the complex. There were some cosmetic upgrades on the exterior and interior of each building. You have to look very hard to see these changes. As a child growing up and living so close to this complex, crime was never an issue. Murders have occurred from the 1970s through the present. Murders were unheard of when I was growing up in the area in the early '70s. Guns didn't seem to be an issue in the early '70s through the late '80s.

We lived on a block that was situated right next to West Park Manor. There were four homes on our block. We played with all the children in The Projects and the families were just nice people. My brothers and sisters had friends in The Projects and my mother and father knew most of the residents. Our home was small and in the early seventies, our family was composed of our mother and nine children. My four older brothers and sisters were born when my mother was married to her husband. We took pride in making our property look nice. It was in our Code of Ethics during this time in history. My mother wasn't married to my father. She was divorced from her husband (Andrew) for whom she had four children. We eventually found out that my mother's husband had tried to kill her because she was going with my father (Malcolm) at that time. She had five children with my father who destroyed her marriage with her husband. Her husband's name was Andrew and my father's name was Malcolm. My father was married to his wife Audrey even though he was going with my mother (Virginia). My father stayed married to his wife while still maintaining an intimate relationship with my mother. He and his wife never had children. During this time, my mother had the ideal family with a husband that was working and they had four children. Her lifestyle was comparable to a middle-income white family. Her husband Andrew was a very hard worker and he held down two jobs. She was sixteen years old when she married her husband. We were trying to figure out why she would give up such a lavish lifestyle and destroy it by going with a married man who forced her to go on welfare. When she was married to Andrew, welfare was never an option.

After my mother's husband tried to kill her in 1955, he didn't succeed. Her husband hit her in the head with a crowbar and placed her in the trunk of his car and took her to South Bend. South Bend was located about six miles from Gary. She almost suffocated in the trunk of his car. Her husband Andrew broke down and told the police where she was. They were able to remove my mother from the trunk of the car before she died. She was able to locate a sharp metal object in the trunk to pierce a hole in the trunk so that she could breathe. Her husband spent fifteen years in prison and he moved to South Bend after he was released from prison. This accident made national headlines around the world.

While her husband was in prison, she had five children with my father and eventually divorced her husband. She continued to have a relationship with my father while he was still married to his wife Audrey. My father's wife knew that my father was in a relationship with my mother, and she knew about the five kids that my father had fathered with my mother. She never left my father, Malcolm. My mother continued in a relationship with my father until she died in 1981 from breast cancer. She was involved with my father from 1950 to 1981, while he was still married to his wife. I still couldn't understand why my mother continued to be in a relationship with a married man after risking her life and almost being murdered by her husband. This is one question that I have been trying to answer after my mother's death. My opinion should have been voiced before she passed and when I was growing up. It bothered me that my father was still married to his wife. My father's wife passed in 2008. My mother never knew that we knew her husband had tried to kill her.

My father was very abusive to my mother and he was an alcoholic for many years during his relationship with her. I can recall telling my mother to leave my father alone as long as he continued to stay married to his wife. She never took our advice. It was such an uncomfortable situation for our family because people knew that our mother was going with a married man. We thought it was a disgrace for our family. My father brought a lot of heartache and tension and chaos to our household. There were periods of my childhood when we would have to hide my mother from my father because of the abuse. She always had black eyes from him punching her. The Gary Police Department would come to our home often to have my father removed from the property and we wanted him locked up. The Gary Police Department knew us all by name because we lived in such a small community. We were in elementary school when these incidents occurred (1960 – 1973). We were too young to help our mother defend herself from my father's attacks. After our father was removed from the home, the police told him not to come back. The police told my father to stay away from this family and leave my mother alone. When we came home from school, my father would be sitting in the living room as if nothing ever happened. We got to a point where we wouldn't call the Gary Police Department anymore because our mother would allow my father to come back to the home after he would be destructive. Our father would always tell us that he was going to kill her. The abuse dissipated as we got older in high school. My father knew we would defend our mother if he tried to lay a hand on her again. When we became teenagers, the abuse dissipated. My father knew that we would retaliate against him.

This situation caused my mother to be on welfare for many years until we all graduated from high school in the late eighties. My father never paid child support for the five children that he fathered with my mother. My mother never forced him to pay child support, and this was something that I couldn't understand. She probably thought that the State of Indiana would cut her welfare check. My father's only concern was maintaining his household with his wife that he lived with in Gary. He did provide and give my mother some assistance with personal things for his children. He did help with clothing for school and the holidays. I think my mother made some kind of agreement with my father by not forcing him to pay child support because her welfare benefits would be cut. That was my take on the situation. One of my brothers made this comment about their situation.

Things were going on in the family that I didn't understand and I couldn't process why my mother allowed my brothers to smoke and bring marijuana into the home. She knew exactly what they were doing because when they were in the basement, the scent of marijuana would be coming out of the heater vents upstairs in our home. Our guests would make comments about the smell and my mother would just ignore their comments. This was when marijuana was illegal. I had this one brother by the name of Randall. He introduced and got a couple of my brothers involved in smoking marijuana. They all started smoking marijuana in the early seventies. I am positive that my brother started my cousins smoking weed as they would refer to it. I never got into drugs or drinking. I am still to this very day puzzled that my mother would allow them to use and bring illegal drugs into the home. I can recall my father making the comment that my mother allowed them to smoke marijuana in the home so that they wouldn't be caught by the police. It would be safer for them to keep this conduct out of sight from any lawful authority. Who would have thought marijuana would eventually be legal as it is today in 2021? So many people participated in smoking weed before it was legal. It seemed to be no big deal unless you were caught by the police. When my brother's friends would visit, they always headed for the basement and I knew this led to smoking marijuana in our basement for years.

Black people just seemed to be involved in unethical and unlawful things in the 1970s and beyond and some parents just sat back and allowed their children to participate in things that would eventually land them in jail or in prison. People seemed to think that smoking marijuana in the 1970s wasn't a serious issue, even though it was illegal. People didn't realize that marijuana leads to doing more serious drugs like cocaine and other illegal drugs. To me, smoking marijuana seemed normal because everybody that I knew was smoking it. I am sure that some parents knew that their children were smoking marijuana and disciplined them accordingly. There were other things that my parents allowed my brothers to do that I thought were disrespectful and drew some red flags. They were allowed to bring girls home and take them to the basement and have sex. My brothers had sex with their girlfriends all the time in our basement. My parents knew what was going on. There were things that I thought were immoral. I wasn't the parent in the home so I didn't have any authority to dictate what was allowed in our household. I wasn't paying the bills, etc. Luckily, none of my brothers got anyone pregnant in high school considering all the sex that was going on in our basement. I know there were times when I would be walking down to the basement and my brother would be having sex with his girlfriend. There were other times when my brother would be having sex with his best friend or some other girl that he went to high school with. If walls could talk, you would hear about other stories that occurred in our basement. For some reason, girls seemed to start taking some form of birth control in high school. It didn't seem that big of a deal. Girls seemed to be more interested in sex than academics. I do recall when a neighbor was asking my mother about getting some kind of birth control. This young girl was in high school during this time.

Another thing that I found unusual was that most of my uncles were married, some of them had girlfriends and this just seemed to be accepted and normal. Some of my uncles were cheating on my aunts. My uncles on my mother's side didn't seem to participate in this kind of behavior. My uncle Ervin was just a God-fearing man and I never knew him to have a girlfriend while married. I thought he was a good role model for my other uncles. Other uncles that didn't partake in this behavior were my Uncle Ben who lived in Chicago and my Uncle Leroy who lived in Gary. My grandfather had girlfriends and cheated on my grandmother. This man wasn't my grandmother's first husband. I can recall an incident in high school when my grandfather propositioned my sister for some sex when he was over to our home. My sister was shocked that he would ask her for sex. When she refused to grant his request, he told my sister that she gave it to everybody else. My sister wasn't a whore and she refused him out of respect and decency. When my grandfather realized that I heard the conversation, he almost had a stroke as I appeared from my bedroom. As a teenager, I never thought he would ask something like this of my sister. I thought it was kind of funny hearing something like this. You have to wonder why so many women tolerated this conduct from men. I am sure that this happened in other areas of the United States. This conduct seemed more prevalent in black communities. I never pursued examining this decorum in some of the other ethnic communities. I don't know what happened in white households because I didn't have that many white friends during my early rearing in Gary. Some blacks were known for having a girlfriend and a wife. It seemed acceptable.

In Gary, people allowed themselves to be involved in certain illegal activities that were spiritually wrong in the eyes of God. I hadn't been involved with other ethnic groups to study some of the immoral things I witnessed in the Black Community. This kind of conduct probably occurred but we probably didn't hear about it. I did have white friends in high school but we never discussed marijuana and they never informed me that their brothers or sisters used pot or any other illegal drugs. I was under the impression that only Blacks smoked marijuana. I was naïve during that time because I am sure that other ethnic groups did drugs and sold drugs in the same manner as Blacks.

Some of these stories might sound very shocking to you but everything that is written in this book is a complete and honest account of what I experienced growing up from 1959 to 1977. There are some personal stories that I will share about people in **Chapter Two** of this book. Some of these stories could have been prevented if some parents would have played more active roles in their child's life. Some children needed more guidance from their parents. Children need direction in life. Some parents directed their attention to other responsibilities but this wasn't an excuse for the neglect or guidance in a child's life. Parents' responsibilities entailed providing for their families and paying their bills.

Some things are better today than they were in the late seventies and to the early 2000s. Some of the same issues that plagued the Black Community back then are still prevalent today. I guess I was just young and didn't think that people would do these things.

I could never understand why my uncles all had girlfriends when they were married to my aunts. Why aren't we having legitimate protests about Blacks killing blacks increasing Black homicide in some cities in the United States? I couldn't understand why crime, poverty, racism are still serious issues in the Black Community. I am still confused and trying to answer some of these questions myself. Why are we still selling drugs and killing each other over drugs? Why are we being killed by cops? Why do we still have some of the highest statistics in crime, poverty, etc.? Why is there a Black Homicide Pandemic? Why do Blacks continue to participate in unlawful things for decades? I have been pondering these thoughts for years even in 2021. I know that some things have improved and I will point these things out in another chapter. I am still trying to figure out what happened to Gary, Indiana; Dayton, Ohio; Chicago, Illinois; Flint, Michigan; Benton Harbor, Michigan; Detroit; Baltimore; New Jersey; and other areas that were thriving in the early seventies and nineties, etc. Why do we still have crime-infested neighborhoods that are predominantly Black? Why are we still victims of crime, dangerous neighborhoods, systemic racism, systemic poverty, welfare, and social injustices? Why are there still so many black men incarcerated? Why do we have the highest percentage of single-parent homes compared to other ethnic groups? I wish I could answer all these questions in a dignified manner. Why are we still dealing with voter suppression? Why is our dignity as human beings still a challenge in America?

I know that it is very hard to lose a child, sister, brother, or relative to a crime. The pain that a parent endures can be incomprehensible. I haven't lost a child but I can imagine the pain and suffering of other people. It is just a part of my well-being and character. Today we have to ask ourselves was there anything that could have been done to prevent the cops from killing these seventy-six black boys and black men? George Floyd, Ahmaud Arbery, Terrance Franklin, Miles Hall, Darius Tarver, William Green, Samuel David Mallard, Kwame "KK" Jones, De'Von Bailey, Christopher Whitfield, Anthony Hill, Eric Logan, Jamarion Slaton, Ryan Twyman, Brandon Webber, Jimmy Atchison, Willie McCoy, Emantic "EJ" Fitzgerald Bradford Jr., D'Ettrick Griffin, Jemel Roberson, DeAndre Ballard, Botham Shem Jean, Robert Lawrence White, Anthony LaMar Smith, Ramarley Graham, Manuel Loggins Jr., Trayvon Martin, Wendell Allen, Kendrec McDade, Larry Jackson Jr., Jonathan Ferrell, Jordan Baker, Victor White III, Dontre Hamilton, Eric Garner, John Crawford, Michael Brown, Ezell Ford, Dante Parker, Kajieme Powell, Laquan McDonald, Akai Gurley, Jamir Rice, Rumain Brishbon, Jerame Reid, Charly Keunang, Tony Robinson, Walter Scott, Freddie Gray, Brendon Glenn, Samual

DuBose, Christian Taylor, Jamar Clark, Mario Woods, Quintonio LeGrier, Gregory Gunn, Akiel Denkins, Alton Sterling, Philando Castile, Terrence Sterling, Terence Crutcher, Keith Lamont Scott, Alfred Olango, Jordan Edwards, Stephon Clark, Danny Ray Thomas, DeJuan Guillory, Patrick Harmon, Jonathan Hart, George Floyd, Maurice Granton, Julius Johnson, Jamee Johnson, and Michael Dean. These deaths have been a tragedy to the Black Community. These questions still linger about their deaths. Can we blame every cop for these deaths? We still need more answers to the sudden death of these African Americans. We are still talking about the sudden death of these African Americans in 2022 and beyond. The most current statistics in 2021 indicate that 105 black men have been killed by the cops. They all have not been listed in this book because the statistics keep fluctuating without an accurate account. Any number that is exposed is very disheartening to the world and the Black Community. Some killings don't get any news coverage or recognition.

Saving a life is one of the most important things in this world. It is just a sad scenario that all these men and boys were killed. We know that there are cops that don't like blacks and all cops aren't bad. There are good cops and bad cops. Life is such a precious gift that we should never take for granted no matter what color we are. This entire book is a true narrative and examination of my black experience in America and a big reflection of my past leading up to the present. I am hoping that it can shed some light on our journey that hasn't always led to the American Dream. We can take things from the past and use them to move forward in the future. Learning is a continuous process. There are a lot of things and tragedies that could have been prevented in our trajectory as human beings. I find it disturbing in some cases as to how we have conducted ourselves as human beings in this world. I hope that you find this book informative and inspiring for future generations and for other ethnic groups to understand our plight in American History. We have been victims of circumstances but we have to take some responsibility for some of the decisions that we have made in this life. Some of these bad decisions have haunted us for decades.

We all have choices in life and when we make bad choices, we have to suffer the consequences. I grew up in a very challenging environment that was good and bad but I decided that I was going to make better choices and I didn't want to end up on welfare again. I can recall my mother giving me a note to take to the grocery store that we had in our neighborhood to give to a store owner asking for credit to buy some food. She told me to tell the store owner that she would pay him when her food stamps came in the mail. Even though we were on welfare, we survived and my mother made sure that we always had something to eat and clothes on our backs. I have some brothers and sisters that made better choices in life and they went to college etc. and fared well in life. There were a couple of my siblings that made some bad choices in life. Some of these bad choices are stated in the narratives. Please don't get the impression that everything that occurred in my life was a tragedy and all sorrow. There were more high points than low points in my life. The people described in my narratives were good and bad people, and they were nice to me growing up. The issues that I had with all of them were some of the choices that they made in life. They decided to make these choices and maybe their environment did contribute to some of their missteps and choices in life. We all will reap what we sow.

Some Blacks have allowed society to write their narrative because of the conduct that they demonstrated throughout their lives. They created situations that weren't conducive to their growth as human beings. They created situations that landed them in jail or prison. I am not categorizing all African Americans. I just wish my cousins, father, my mother, my sister, and a few brothers would have made better choices in life. We have allowed others to be storytellers and tell our stories based on the preferences that we have made throughout history. I made sure that I was going to tell my story and not allow the influences in society to dictate how my story was going to unfold in life. I decided what my destiny would be when I was a child. I had the ambition and desire to accomplish things in life and that is what I did. I have no regrets about some of the decisions that I made. I made a few mistakes also.

So many cities that were composed of black communities began to decline because of white flight and jobs left these cities. Drugs were planted in black neighborhoods which led to the decline of some neighborhoods. Blacks were enticed by these drugs and wound up selling drugs for fast cash and other reasons. Foundries started to pack up and leave black communities such as manufacturing, the automobile industry, and the steel mills started to decline. Financial distress became a disease in so many black communities. Whites left these communities in droves and left cities struggling to survive. Cities suffered in Michigan, Wisconsin, Illinois, Texas, Mississippi, and other urban areas in the United States. Unemployment can destroy a state and a city, people lose their sense of self-worth when they are jobless which leads to higher crime rates and other disasters that inflict communities. These states were vibrant and prosperous when there was plenty of jobs etc. I could have focused on other cities that have the same dynamics as Gary, Indiana.

So many stereotypes have become a major disease for so many struggling Black Communities. Some of these stereotypes still hold to this very day in 2021. Some of the stereotypes have dissipated. All ethnic groups experience some afflictions and problems but Blacks seem to have more issues compared to other ethnic groups. When there are issues with some ethnic group, this becomes an issue for the entire world. When it is all said and done, we all need each other no matter what nationality we are or creed or color. We are so much stronger as a nation when we stick together and lend a hand to others. We should never allow race to be the determining factor when other ethnic groups are in need or suffering. Some whites have been very instrumental in addressing the hardships and needs of Blacks. President Kennedy, Jimmy Carter, Lyndon Johnson addressed issues that were negative in Black Communities and they did try to come up with some solutions. I can recall when Jimmy Carter was president, there were summer programs that existed in black communities and I took advantage of these programs and worked all the way through high school. There were some good job initiatives when Democrats were presidents.

Please remember that as you read through this book, this was the most current data available on statistics, etc. Some statistics are the most current available and data does fluctuate over the years. My sources were taken from research that was readily available on the Internet. My research targets issues that I felt were important to the Black Community and my convictions about myself and African Americans. My point-of-view is discussed and supported by research and my personal experiences in life. This information was gathered from thousands of hours of research done and conducted online during the Coronavirus Pandemic (2019 – Present) when libraries were closed and not open to the public. I am a research specialist and it was so exciting gathering this information and turning the information into a readable and informational manuscript that I hope we all can read and appreciate its value to the world.

Chapter Two

Factors That Have Contributed to the Hardships of Some Blacks

The focus of this chapter is to focus on some of the factors that led to blacks making very poor decisions by getting involved with illegal drugs during the early '60s and in the 2000s. The selling and usage continued for decades in low underprivileged areas around the United States. Marijuana came to the United States in the 1930s but the trend of using it flourished in the early '60s. It has been said that black neighborhoods were saturated with marijuana and other illegal drugs during the sixties which initiated use and selling. Selling marijuana was a quick way to earn some fast cash. What some people didn't understand is that using marijuana would lead to using more potent drugs like crack cocaine and other illegal drugs. There is an opioid epidemic in the United States today. People were tempted to sell drugs because they lived in low-income areas. They wanted quick cash. Other factors contributed to some of the hardships of African Americans and other people of color like, Systemic Racism, Welfare, Poverty, and living in very dangerous neighborhoods. Marijuana became legal in some states at the beginning of 2018 and we began to see a decrease in arrests for possession by African Americans. This chapter is focusing on the history and blacks' involvement in drugs that caused them to go to jail and prison etc.

Marijuana

Marijuana has a long history of human use. The original plan and content were used as herbal medicine not to get high. It originated in Asia around 500 B.C. Marijuana was used for other things during this period by early colonists who grew hemp for textiles and rope. They weren't thinking about using this drug for personal reasons to get high or get involved in anything that might be illegal. It was just like a normal plant grown in the fields.

The legal aspect of marijuana has changed over the years. In the 20th Century, political and racial factors led to the criminalization of marijuana in the United States. The plant was developed in Central Asia before it hit Africa, Europe, and America. The hemp fiber had many uses, making clothing, paper, sails, and rope. The seeds were used as food.

The plant was fast-growing and easy to process with its many uses. Farmers were required to grow the hemp plant in the early 1600s. During the early discovery of hemp plants, they have low levels of tetrahydrocannabinol (THC) a chemical that gave users mind-altering effects. It would give people a feeling of being high. Marijuana has the psychoactive properties of the cannabis plant. It has been proven that some varieties of marijuana have higher levels of THC for healing practices.

Marijuana has been used for many purposes since its discovery. This would include medical purposes, recreational weed where people used the drug to get high. It would allow you to maintain a mild high for hours. It was sold in the form of cannabis extracts to pharmacies and doctor's offices in Europe and the United States for stomach problems and other ailments in the late 1800s. They also used it to treat Cholera. People were burning the seeds and inhaling the smoke before processing the plant into something that resembled a cigarette. People developed a marijuana addiction, especially in the early 1930s.

The United States wasn't feeling comfortable with the use of marijuana. This led to the development of the Marijuana Tax Act of 1937. It was the first federal U.S. law to punish people nationwide for using marijuana and selling marijuana. Industrial uses of this plant were considered not illegal. A person was caught selling marijuana in 1937. This individual was sentenced to four years of hard labor. A stricter punishment came later.

Marijuana – The Effects

Marijuana has some side effects that include both mental and physical. Most of the effects have been short-term which include euphoria, mood swings, increased appetite, and heightened sensory perception. There might be other properties of this drug that weren't discussed in the development of this drug when it started to turn up in the United States.

One thing that I noticed about users was mood changes and increased appetite for sweet things. Everything seemed funny to them even if you thought that they weren't. Their eyes became red and bloodshot and they had a glassy glow to them. It was obvious when they smoked pot because the scent was in their clothing. The scent is very strong and I think smells worse than cigarettes. If you walked into a room, you would know automatically that someone was smoking marijuana. The smell is very distinctive. You don't confuse it with another smell especially cigarettes or smoking a cigar.

Smokable marijuana evolved in the United States after the Mexican Revolution of 1910 to 1911. It became known as colored people's drug well into the 1960s as the baby boomers discovered it. White college kids began to smoke it and it lost its racial connotations. For some strange reason, I always thought that blacks smoked and sold marijuana. Marijuana turned up in New Orleans and other areas that were highly populated by blacks. Sailors and sometimes immigrants from the Caribbean brought cannabis to the United States. The stereotype was placed on blacks right away because of their use which eventually led to selling the drug for quick money and white people did not. It was stated that blacks and Mexicans used this drug more than any other ethnic group.

This helped feed into the racist fears and stereotypes that were used to make marijuana illegal in the 1930s. The more blacks used the drug, the more it became illegal. This drug caused a lot of blacks to be incarcerated for years in prisons. There also was speculation that blacks used this drug to seduce white women. Society is trying to right the wrong that caused so many blacks to be charged with possession of marijuana by making it legal in some states around 2018. People have been fighting to make it legal for years.

My brothers, cousins, and their friends smoked marijuana but I didn't think that my parents ever used this drug. They grew up in the 1930s when the drug was somewhat popular for some teenagers and adults. I guess they didn't have any desire to smoke pot.

We know that white hippies enjoyed smoking marijuana during the Beatles' Era. This was a known fact and most Americans didn't seem to think it was a big deal. My parents smoked cigarettes and they did drink alcoholic beverages. It became a big deal when blacks started to smoke the drug and sell the drug. It was just another excuse to lock up blacks.

My honest opinion is that marijuana should have never been illegal since it was used for medical purposes in the late '60s and today it is used for medical ailments. So many blacks were caught selling the drug and served minimal sentences. By making it illegal, it was a tactic to incarcerate blacks because they were heavy users of marijuana and they did sell the drug. My brothers knew where to buy this drug and they knew who sold the drug. There are some concerns with it being legal today. We hope that people will not drive under the influence of marijuana. It can cause some serious accidents and a host of other personal issues that affect the mind when a person is high. I have seen people roll joints that look like cigarettes. I have seen people buy a nickel bag of pot. This is how most blacks purchased the drug.

One thing that I noticed about marijuana when my brothers would buy the drug, they would purchase it from users. There was never one person that sold the drug. It just seemed so easy to buy. When they did use the drug, you would always see the same people gather to smoke the drug. These were people that my brothers went to school with and they hung around people that were in the same grade as they were. There were occasions when I was just hanging out in the basement with my brothers and their friends would come over and sometimes my cousins would be over to our house. The people that participated in using the drug, all knew how to roll a joint as they would refer to when they had a nickel bag of the drug.

Status:

Marijuana is legal in most states in the United States. This drug has made progress in treating certain medical issues in patients that have very serious diseases. People that have had chemotherapy have used this drug and benefited from it for medical reasons. This was also a positive step for blacks since so many of them were charged with selling the drug.

Crack Cocaine

Crack cocaine is a crystallized form of cocaine. It became popular in the 1980s. This is the time that some blacks started using the drug heavily. They graduated from marijuana and started using crack cocaine. People knew that there was more money in selling cocaine. Crack cocaine was produced by dissolving powdered cocaine in a mixture of water and ammonia and boiling it down until a solid chunk was formed. It was broken down into smaller chunks or rocks and then smoked. I can remember catching my brothers and some of their friends in my kitchen processing crack cocaine for smoking. When they would refer to buying a rock, I never knew what they were referring to was crack cocaine. They were buying a rock of crack cocaine. I was very naive about drugs growing up in the '70s.

They used crack cocaine because it was cheaper and the high was more intense and the crack was more addictive than regular powdered cocaine. You could buy a rock for five dollars. The reason that crack cocaine is so addictive is because your first high is said to be the best high that you will ever receive and this is what hooks the user. So many drug users go through life trying to achieve that very first high for many years. This keeps the addiction going. In some cases, drug users never achieve that first high ever again in life. This is why my brother is still addicted to crack cocaine after thirty years.

Crack usage had a big surge between 1985 and 1989. Users jumped from 4.2 million to 5.8 million people. During this period, crime increased in major black cities around the world. My brother almost went to prison during this time for the possession of crack cocaine. I mentioned this in **Chapter Three**, he managed to beat the criminal charges against him with a very good lawyer. There are still blacks today incarcerated for selling crack cocaine. The punishment is more severe than selling marijuana. During the height of the cocaine crisis, there were 32 percent of homicides and 60 percent of drug-related homicides in New York City. Blacks were incarcerated at higher levels than whites and other ethnic groups. Crack and cocaine is a drug that is used by everybody and not just blacks. Blacks just seem to be the target for drug-related crimes. The selling of crack cocaine was very detrimental to black communities.

Status:

Crack cocaine and crack are still illegal today and I am sure that this will never change unless they can find some kind of way to market the drug and sell it in drugstores for some kind of medical purpose. I have more issues with this drug than some of the other drugs like marijuana etc.

Systemic Racism

Racism is always going to be an issue and a part of the American fabric. It has existed in our society since the development of slavery in the early 1600s. Racism is like an infectious disease that has caused harm to certain groups of people with suspicion or to attribute negative characteristics to an entire group of people especially African Americans.

This evil has manifested itself in people's thoughts for decades. We still have continuing inequalities in education, housing, employment, wealth, and the representation in leadership positions by our country's shameful history and systemic racism. This issue today seems to still have some impact on African Americans and other people of color in a negative manner. America has succumbed to a disease that should have been eradicated years ago. People still perpetuate the same stereotypes about people of color with blacks at the top of the list.

Discrimination is solely based on race and ethnicity. We can say that the United States has made some progress in eradicating some institutional, legalized racial discrimination, Jim Crow laws, "separate but equal" schools, voting, and owning property. There have been some minor victories for African Americans.

We still have much work to do to change the scenario and dynamics of the past. We can examine the data on social and economic welfare displaying disparities between African Americans, other ethnic groups, and their white counterparts.

African Americans, Latinos, and Native Americans still have higher unemployment rates than the national average. This affects minorities, their income, inequality affects blacks more than whites.

When you examine the median wealth in the United States, in white households, their wealth is ten times greater than blacks and eight times greater than Hispanics.

The data still indicates that minority homeownership is behind whites and minorities face many challenges trying to secure a mortgage.

The data also shows the discrepancies in the Criminal Justice system between African Americans and Latinos. They are treated unfairly despite the evidence that shows whites committing crimes at the same rates as blacks and other people of color.

African Americans and other minorities live in some of the worse communities in the United States because our society is so homogenous. This takes away the opportunity for us to learn from others and interact with people who are ethnically different. Diversity strengthens our communities. Diversity is the landmark that makes this world so homogeneous for all people.

Many minority groups and people of color are living in low-income areas and their access to quality schools, safe neighborhoods, reliable transportation, or higher-paying jobs is still limited compared to whites. Violence, crime, and drugs have affected low-income areas in a negative manner which has caused the demise of some black families and other people of color. We have been forced to do things that weren't considered normal in the land of opportunity.

We as Americans need a provocative plan to end systemic racism because it will continue to be the Achilles heel for African Americans and other people of color. We need to work as a team to combat this disease that has had such a profound impact on African Americans and other people of color. We need to work together as a nation to continue to eradicate systemic racism. Today, we are more aware of how it has affected our race and other people of color. As I began to get older, I noticed some of the discrepancies that have led to the suffering of African Americans because of some of the policies of white America.

Systemic Poverty and Welfare

Poverty affected blacks and whites in the 1960s. This would also include every religion and national origin. Blacks weren't the only ones that benefited from welfare and Aid to Dependent Children (ADC). Around the 1960s, 35 million Americans needed some kind of assistance from the federal government. It was assumed that blacks needed more assistance than any other ethnic minorities as well as other people of color.

Lyndon B. Johnson was the residing president during this time. Johnson chose white people to represent poverty to the American public because if he would have just chosen only to represent black families, Congress wouldn't pass any kind of legislature to give federal assistance to African Americans. The bill would have stalled in Congress. He needed support from Republicans and Democrats to pass any kind of welfare legislation. Republicans have always been against any kind of welfare legislation when it was targeted to help only minorities and people of color. President Johnson had to convince the white elected officials to help poor people that they thought were like them, meaning white Americans. Republicans have always labeled welfare as a form of socialism.

During the welfare era, there are still lingering questions about the validity of this movement and society has always used this as a snare against African Americans because they have assumed that welfare was created for blacks only. The literature doesn't support that idea.

When Blacks lived in the South during the 1960s, it was harder to receive ADC during the harvest season of crops because they wanted them to work in the fields for any kind of assistance. The South did everything that they could to discourage black women from welfare rolls. They were disqualified if they had a man living in their home who wasn't their husband and if their homes didn't meet the expectations and guidelines of the assigned Social Worker. A prime example of how ADC worked was demonstrated in the movie *Claudine* with Diahann Carroll and James Earl Jones in 1974. This movie reminded me of my household around this time. My mother had five children and we were on Aid For Dependent Children. My mother took advantage of this program until we all graduated from high school in the early '80s.

Blacks began to migrate to the North where they were most successful at obtaining welfare benefits from the federal government. This program was tied to the Civil Rights Movement of 1955 through 1968. The federal government began administering anti-poverty programs in the 1960s because of Lyndon B. Johnson's work on poverty. This made it very difficult for states to deny aid. It was very hard for states to discriminate against certain ethnic groups and this would include blacks. The number of blacks on the welfare rolls started to climb in the North and South in the early '60s throughout the 1980s.

My mother moved from the South in the early '60s with most of her siblings which included sisters. Some of her sisters moved to New York. Her brothers stayed in the South. I thought that my mother moved North to secure better opportunities. Her intent wasn't to jump on the welfare rolls because she found a husband and started a family. Her husband was working and providing for the family. So many blacks that moved North jumped on the welfare train. When my mother divorced her husband, she became one of the passengers on the welfare train. She stayed on that train for many decades. She remained on welfare until her last child graduated from high school around 1983.

When we were on welfare, we did apply for many programs that kept us afloat during some of our most vulnerable times growing up in Gary, Indiana. There were grants that we could apply for that would assist with going to college along with work-study. This assistance made it possible for me to attend a four-year university and graduate with a degree in education. After graduation, I was able to attend graduate school and obtain a master's degree. It was important to take advantage of these opportunities, and some of my other brothers benefited from these opportunities as well.

It was kind of a negative experience for me being on welfare but it did allow the family to survive and we were allowed to apply for financial aid for college. The thing that bothered me the most was that my cousins weren't on welfare. We never discussed welfare with the people that we knew or went to school with. The perception was very negative if your friends knew that you were on any kind of government assistance. It was taboo for families that were able to survive without ADC. My cousins' parents were always working and for some strange reason, they seem to have more things than we had. This was just my analysis of the situation. They seem to always have new bicycles and we didn't have any.

Their families went on more trips during the summer when school was out. In hindsight, I wish my mother would have made better choices. This is what it comes down to in life. Some people needed some kind of assistance because of the turmoil that was caused by the family structure. My mother was very capable of obtaining a decent job in the same manner that her sisters did. She could have gotten a full-time job and avoided any government help.

There were reforms in the 1980s and the 1990s that imposed work requirements on recipients of welfare or ADC that received cash assistance. In 1996, the federal government restricted the amount of time that people could receive benefits and required a certain percentage of welfare recipients to be working while receiving some assistance. This was encouraging news to me because this would alleviate the problem of so many people applying for assistance that were healthy, capable to work full-time jobs like other normal human beings. Some people have abused these privileges by the government by having more children to increase their assistance. There are people in society that didn't have any alternatives but to accept welfare from the federal government. There was no reason that my mother couldn't have accepted or obtained a job in the same manner that her sisters did when they moved to Indiana from the North. Welfare became a crutch for so many blacks in the early '60s. Some of them did want handouts and they didn't want to work.

We know that in reality some people are just born in poverty, not by choice. It just happens to some of the most unfortunate people in our society and that included some black families throughout history. Blacks have always seemed to have higher numbers in poverty and some might be considered abusers of free government assistance. There have been other issues that have drawn them to welfare that have been discussed over the years. Welfare continues to be a major stereotype for our people, especially when so many families have been recipients of some kind of government assistance throughout the years. You have heard the stereotype that most blacks don't want to work when the federal government is giving out free handouts and welfare. Some of these comments might be validated and some might be bogus. It depends on who these issues are discussed with. It does seem that most of these stereotypes are perpetuated by some white Americans. All white Americans don't feel this way about blacks.

Please understand that we weren't poor. My mother decided to accept welfare even though my father was working a full-time job every day but he was still married to his wife and going with my mother. There was no reason for my mother to be on any kind of welfare because she was intelligent and she could hold down a very good job. This goes back to my analysis of choices and choices had consequences. All of my cousins' mothers and fathers both had full-time jobs and welfare was never an issue in their households. It was embarrassing when people at school knew that you were on welfare because everyone that attended school in Gary, Indiana was on some kind of assistance. As I said before that my mother had a beautiful home and was married to her husband that was working two jobs and he also kept his children working in the summer. Her lifestyle was very lavish when she was married. You would think why would she want to sabotage her somewhat middle-class lifestyle and get involved with a married man who wasn't paying child support for fathering five children with her. It would have been nice to have two parents all the time.

Black Wealth Inequality

There is evidence of astonishing racial disparities among whites and blacks in the United States. This has been going on for decades. The typical net worth of a typical white family is nearly ten times greater than that of a Black family. The gap in wealth between Blacks and whites from 2016 to the present indicates the accumulated inequality and discrimination. There is a difference in power and opportunity that is reflected in America.

We are living in a society where the wealth gap illustrates a society where Blacks have been left behind in inequality and opportunities that have been afforded to other ethnic groups especially white citizens.

Blacks have been trying to build wealth throughout American history. These efforts have been repressed because of 246 years of tangible slavery and mismanagement of the Freedman's Savings Bank. This was referred to as the "Black Wall Street." The discrimination policies throughout the 20th Century, Jim Crow Laws limiting many opportunities in southern states, the GI Bill, the New Deal's Fair Labor Standards Act's exemption of domestic agriculture and service occupations, and redlining. The wealth was taken from southern states before it had the opportunity to grow.

We need to look at how persistent the wealth gap is between Black households and white households. The chart below shows the median net worth for white households has far surpassed that of Black households through recessions over the last thirty years. It is easier to see movements in white wealth on a much larger scale. When we experienced a financial crisis or economic depression, the median net worth showed a decline by more Black families (44.3 percent decline from 2007 to 2013) than for white families (26.1 percent decline). The wealth of white families compared to the wealth of Black families is higher today than that at the start of the century.

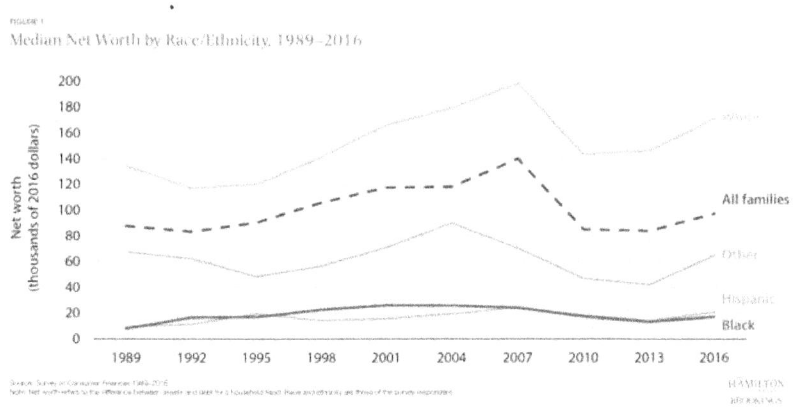

Median wealth is the wealth of the household in the middle of a distribution—demonstrates the experience of a typical family. It does not show the amount of wealth that is held by the richest households in the United States. The average white wealth in the states is ($929,800) influenced by rich families which is 6.7 times greater than blacks' average wealth ($138,100).

For some reason or another, white adults tend to be older around fifty-five years of age than African Americans forty-nine years old. It has been proven that older white adults seem to have more wealth. The eighteen- to thirty-four-year-olds of both races have little wealth. The gap rises quickly with sixty-five- to seventy-four-year-olds, it accumulates to $302,500 in median white wealth, and $46,890 in median Black wealth. Wealth is very important to every houschold in the United States no matter what race you are. It is our survival mechanism that is entitled to every living American citizen. It determines our worth in society. Households can have the same income, but the household with fewer expenses and more accumulated wealth from other assets will have more wealth and chances of survival in a greed-driven society. The racial wealth gap remains even for families with the same income according to the research and some economists that research wealth disparity. For people in the top ten percent by income (only 3.6 percent Black), racial wealth inequality is still very large. The median net worth for white families in this income group is $1,789,300 compared to $343,160 for African American families. Racial gaps still exist in every income group except the bottom quintile (23.5 percent Black) where median net worth is zero for everyone.

It is a known fact that higher income and higher wealth have always favored white families compared to the wealth and income of Black families with the same incomes. One reason was determined to verify that statement is that white families receive larger inheritances on average than black families. Economists have determined that inheritances and intergenerational transfers account for more of the racial gap than any other demographic and socioeconomic indicators among and intergenerational transfers account for more of the racial gap than any other demographic and Blacks and whites. Also, high- and middle-income Black families are more likely than whites to be solicited to assist family members and neighbors. This was something that I experienced growing up. My mother was always trying to provide some support to her sisters. This still exists today in many Black families around the world and deprived areas of the United States where many Blacks live. Some Black families are looking out for handouts and some financial assistance from their relatives. Some families depend highly on their grandparents for some kind of assistance.

We have just discussed some important factors that play a role in the wealth gap between Blacks and whites throughout history. Wealth is a safety net to conquer setbacks and loss of income from work and unemployment. Other factors can contribute to the demise of income that is beyond our control. A safety net allows us to take risks that we wouldn't normally take. The right family wealth allows families especially young people entering into the labor force to have access to housing in safe neighborhoods with good schools paving the way for prospects of their children.

Wealth brings on many challenges and opportunities. It allows being entrepreneurs and inventors of their products. The income from wealth is taxed at much lower rates than the income that we obtain from working a regular job.

Work income is heavily taxed and this is something that we all experience before retirement.

There is no simple explanation for the wealth disparity among Black Americans and White Americans. We can examine some differences in educational attainment and tax policy. It has been proven that white families tend to have higher levels of debt as compared to other ethnic groups reading through the literature. They still surpass Blacks and other ethnic groups in wealth equity. Their wealth equity has always surpassed the wealth equity of African Americans.

Some things can be changed in society but erasing financial disparities is a challenge for most economists and others who have challenged this problem. One approach that has been alluded to is reform on the taxation of income from wealth. The income from inheritances and wealth, in general, is taxed at an inequitable low rate when compared to earnings. We can try to be optimistic in the future about erasing some of the wealth disparities.

As we go through and experience life, disparities are always going to exist among people in some form or fashion. Blacks seem to be affected more frequently by financial disparities more than any other race on the planet. We can focus on trying to eradicate the status quote with some perseverance and encouragement. We should focus our energy on the things that we can change so that future generations will fare better than some of our predecessors. There are always going to be challenges for each generation of Black Americans and we have to look forward to the challenges that are ahead.

Wealth has become abundantly important especially during the Coronavirus pandemic because so many African Americans suffered severely from this pandemic especially black women. So many of them owned their businesses during such a devastating time for people of color. We know that wealth is the difference between what families own and this would include their savings and checking accounts, retirement savings, houses and cars, and what they owe on credit cards, student loans, and mortgages, among other debt. As I stated earlier, Black households have a fraction of the wealth of white households, leaving them dire financial situations when a serious crisis strikes and with fewer economic opportunities than some white households. It is a known fact that wealth allows households to weather a financial emergency such as a layoff or a family illness. An illness can add up to serious medical bills when a person doesn't have health insurance.

The pandemic brought on multiple emergencies to American families across all demographics including white households. Blacks did experience the lack of financial security combined with disproportionate exposure to the deadly coronavirus that imposed disastrous results for the Black Community. We are still dealing with the ramifications of the virus financially in 2021. Please remember that wealth also provides the revenues for Blacks to invest in their children's education, to start a business, relocate for new and better opportunities in another state, buy a house, buy a car, and have the opportunity to participate in the democratic process. Blacks have suffered in education because many households in Black communities cannot afford to pay for reliable internet or electronic devices to facilitate remote learning as compared to more suburban districts in the United States. President Barack Obama created an initiative to have internet access in every household in the United States. The playing field for so many financial issues has taken its toll and negatively made opportunities for Blacks off-balanced.

Black Homicide in America (Past and Present)

The statistic for black homicide is very alarming when compared to the homicide of other ethnic groups in the world. We know that drug and gun-infested neighborhoods breed crime, violence, and death. According to the FBI, African Americans accounted for 52.4 percent of all homicide offenders in 2018, with Whites 43.1 percent, other/Unknown 4.4 percent. Of these, 15.4 percent were Hispanic or Latino. The per-capita offending rate for African Americans was roughly six times higher than whites, and the victim rate is a similar figure.

We are dealing with a sad reality with a black homicide that has invaded many black communities for decades. Homicide is occurring in major cities like Baltimore, Chicago, Gary, Flint, Benton Harbor, and other predominantly black communities around the world. In the year 2020 more than 300 people were killed in the streets of Baltimore, just about all of the deaths were African Americans. I do recall visiting Baltimore around 1983 and it was a scary time walking around in Baltimore. I was killing time after an interview before I was about to leave the city on a plane. For some strange reason, I was on guard because of the crime in the city during this time. I feared that someone would try and rob me all dressed up in a nice suit. As I was parading in the area, a cab driver stopped and told me to be careful. He said that I might be a target for crime and he said that I should go to the airport and not wait in Baltimore. I got into the cab and he took me to the airport. This cab driver feared for my safety in Baltimore before I returned to Gary, Indiana.

For some strange reason, we have to realize that some black people are more susceptible threats to other black people than the Ku Klux Klan or the White Citizens' Council. It is very difficult to say this as an African American male about our race and people. We are being gunned down in the streets by other blacks that align with our memories of the many blacks lynched in communities across the United States after Reconstruction.

It has been determined that black homicide is a devastating plague severely affecting black communities across the country. Blacks shouldn't be killing anyone let alone their race.

These killings continued in the present as the country continued to face the coronavirus pandemic that placed the governors in some states to issue stay-at-home lockdowns. People were supposed to stay at home unless they needed essentials such as groceries and prescription medications etc. You would have thought that the killings would stop. The killings didn't stop and again it was mostly black victims.

People are afraid to admit that some of the aggressive law enforcement techniques have worked to reduce crime in Baltimore and other black communities where the homicide rate is higher. People objected to the stop-and-frisk practice in New York that was created by the former mayor, Michael Blumberg. It did result in a decline in homicides in the city during this period in history. Richmond, Virginia got tough on gun violations and the homicide rate decreased. When they did allow gun violations to be prosecuted as federal crimes, guilty persons were sent to federal prisons in places like Utah. The majority of these people were African Americans.

A turning point in Baltimore and other cities came when some mayors got tough on "bad guys with guns," homicides went down. The people that were detained were black. As you look at these reductions in homicides, the people that benefited most were African Americans who lost fewer sons, daughters, fathers, and mothers to unnecessary street violence. The question that we are asking ourselves is how to address the bad behavior of some blacks without defaming the "whole" black community? Some people continue to struggle to give a balanced and positive picture of black life in America. It is a known fact that some black people do bad things. We can also say that other races do bad things too. The sad thing about black homicide is that their victims are most often black people. You keep asking yourself, why are we killing each other? Blacks shouldn't be killing each other or anyone else in the world. Death is such a horrible reality when it affects our people.

When we examine the attitude toward bad guys with guns is not the same in these violent neighborhoods, where you fear for your life every day compared to relatively peaceful suburbs where crime is a minor issue. Our communities are under siege by black gun-packing criminals. At a town hall meeting in a black community, a young black woman couldn't understand why her brother's killer had remained free on the street awaiting trial for a previous gun violation. So many people accused of murder in cities have existing gun violations. We have got to break this cycle.

We are at the crossroads of our existence as African Americans, we must reconcile, black pride, civil liberties, and civil rights as we focus on creating more safe black communities. We don't want to resort to stop-and-frisk policies or mass incarceration, but something like it may be needed. These efforts can focus on illegal weapons pretty much the same as stop-and-frisk efforts at major airports. This doesn't seem to be a problem in the large White and Asian communities. It is in the black communities and must be addressed as a particular problem to those black neighborhoods around the world.

Gun violence is a major problem in some black communities along with selling illegal drugs that have led to the demise of many African Americans. I will never forget the incident in Gary where my best friend was looking for his son. He found him in an alley dead from a drug deal gone bad. He was shot in the head. This predatory behavior should not continue or be tolerated as we look ahead into the future and beyond 2021. We need to understand that this lawlessness victimizes black families, the black community, and future generations. As an African American, at some point, we need to stop letting the presumed rights of a few blacks endanger the lives of many. Our integrity and well-being are vital to the world and the black community.

Comments:

I strongly object to gun violence and the selling of illegal drugs. We are killing each other over things that have no value in this life. Human life is sustainable but drugs and guns are not. The value of human life exceeds everything that this world has to offer. We need to value our existence as well as others. This would include all ethnic groups. When guns are used for violence and other inappropriate things, our fabric in America is compromised. Homicide is very serious and it should never take place during a pandemic exposing innocent people.

As we continue our journey in this book, I hope that you can walk away with some positive aspects that you can apply to live by as it exists in the 21st Century. We all have made mistakes in life and we will continue to make mistakes as long as we are on this earth. We can't dwell on the past but we can take aspects of the past to improve our well-being in a positive and conducive manner. This book is just a referendum of things that I experienced and things that I thought were wrong living in a world where I thought we all had the opportunity to pursue the American Dream no matter what our dreams entailed.

Race Riots (1960 – Present)

As we go back in time, we can remember riots during the Civil Rights Era and the assassination of Dr. Martin Luther King in 1968 in Birmingham, Alabama. The 1960s' riots had a significant negative impact on blacks' income and employment from 1960 to 1980. These riots destroyed and significantly depressed the median value of black-owned properties, neighborhoods between 1960 and 1970 with no resurgence in the 1970s.

People can recall the race-related riots that had such a profound impact throughout United States cities in the 1960s which resulted in injuries, deaths, and arrests as well as considerable property damage in predominantly black areas. The United States has experienced race-related disturbances throughout history. These riots led to some assistance from the National Guard and other military units when necessary. Some of the deadliest riots took place in Detroit (1967), Los Angeles (1965), and Newark (1967). The severity of these riots included arrests, injuries, and arson.

After the death of Dr. Martin Luther King Jr., the riots became less planned, less organized, less orchestrated, and nonviolent demonstrations of the Civil Rights Movement. Social scientists have studied the reasons for riots for many years with conflicting views leading up to the 2000s. They have focused on the economic impact that riots have had on African Americans and cities where these riots have occurred. These riots affected blacks' income and employment and when looting is involved, the impact of the riots is very severe. They are a detriment to the welfare and well-being of African Americans in a negative fashion.

During this period in history (1960 – 1980) earnings were low for black males without full-time work. This placed a very serious burden on the black family for years. Blacks were susceptible to living in high-poverty urban neighborhoods as poverty began to take its toll. Residential segregation also led to more poor socioeconomic outcomes for blacks. The question has been to detect whether riots lead to the economic demise that destroyed employment opportunities, incomes, and property values of African Americans. The literature implies that the riots significantly hurt the median value of the black-owned property between 1960 and 1970 with no rebound in the 1970s. What we should realize as African Americans is that riots destroy the property values in our communities. If you drove through Gary, my perception would be seen in full color because of the destruction in some of the neighborhoods that still linger on in 2021. These images are not exaggerated and this imagery can be seen in other black communities in the United States.

As we proceed to 1980 through the 2000s, there has been a nationwide protest against police killings of African Americans with the recent deaths of Eric Garner, George Floyd, and other blacks. Black rebellion, defiance, and protests are more frequent today with more peaceful demonstrations, looting, and violent riots. This behavior has spread across the country because of police behavior, the brutality of Breonna Taylor, and Ahmaud Arbery. These unexpected deaths of African Americans occurred when the police kicked the hornet's nest and opened up the flood gates for blacks to behave unconventionally and violent tone against cops. Other ethnic groups have joined in to support blacks because of treatment by the police force. Decent people were protesting the brutal treatment of African Americans. The United States Constitution does allow protests that are not non-violent, peaceful, and nonthreatening in 2019 to the present.

These protests allowed opportunists to take advantage of a serious situation where the intent was to involve people in a peaceful protest to express the outrage of police brutality against African Americans. Looters had no business participating in activities that destroyed businesses and other important properties in certain areas where the riots were taking place. Blacks rose against the cops because of the killings by police as I mentioned earlier. Freedom marches can be successful with the right intent and focus just as long as these marches relate to the civil-rights era as a movement of nonviolence and civil disobedience according to the standards of Dr. Martin Luther King Jr. and other Civil Rights leaders, past and present. Violence leads to the destruction of property, loss of human life, and other casualties of a city or region. Violence usually leads to unexpected death and hardship for many people. When we all work together in harmony in a positive manner, so many goals can be achieved that are reflective of the cause.

Throughout history, black people have demonstrated violence, nonviolence, marches, protests, and boycotts because of the treatment by society. God didn't intend for some of these hardships to happen. Many blacks feel that they need to express their dissent and rebellion when they feel that they have been mistreated by a society that offers the American Dream to everyone. Blacks do understand a righteous rebellion: Violence initiates a response whether negative or positive. It does interfere with the status quo and societal norms.

We have to remember that looting destroys businesses, neighborhoods, and has a detrimental financial impact on a city or neighborhood that has limited resources for the residents. It changes the dynamics of the situation and the blame is placed in the laps of some African Americans who are involved in this kind of conduct. It perpetuates the stereotype that some blacks are thugs and hoodlums in a given area of the United States. All wars seem to be won with violence. What Blacks are doing today is participating in a nationwide rebellion revolution allowing blacks to express their frustrations with some of the criminal law practices in the United States. They want the same treatment that is afforded other ethnic groups in the Land of the Free without any interference from our established legal system in the United States.

Police Killing Blacks

It is a known fact that police have been killing blacks in larger proportions than in previous years due to crime and the treatment of blacks. The death of Rodney King caused riots and other casualties to Los Angeles and other cities that housed black communities on March 3, 1991. Blacks are well-represented among people being killed by police unarmed. The census indicates that blacks make up 12 percent of the general population in the United States. It is a known fact that 26 percent of blacks are killed by police in predominantly black communities. The Census acknowledges that whites make up the majority of lethal force (50%) from 2015-2019. They currently are the majority of the population (61%). Asians have less-lethal force by police making up 5 percent of the general population with 2 percent of force by police. Hispanics are 18 percent of the general population with 18 percent of lethal force by police. Native Americans make up 1 percent of the general population and 1.7 percent of victims by lethal force by the police. (See Chart Below)

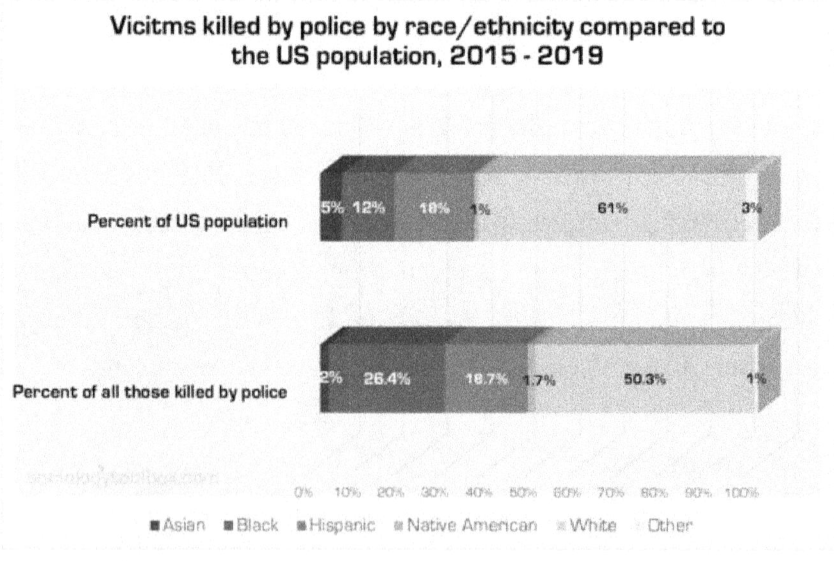

It is terrible to think that one ethnic group exceeds lethal force by police with a lower percentage representation in the

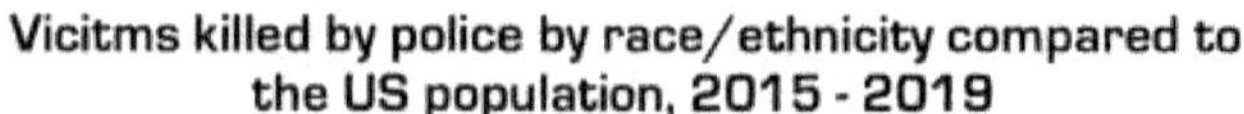

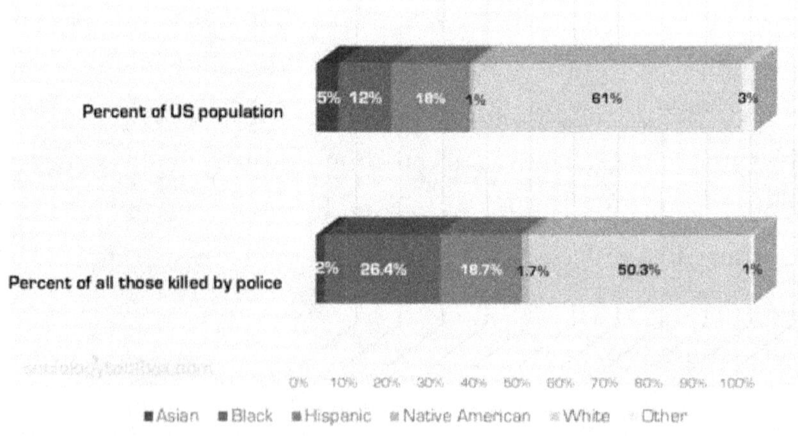

general population. We have to ask ourselves, why do we have so many encounters with the police that become lethal?

The chart below shows the over and under-representation of ethnic groups from 2015 to 2019 in comparison to victims of lethal police encounters to the proportion to U.S. population estimates. Black has been over-represented in lethal force by police compared to whites, Hispanics, Native Americans, and Asian Americans. (See Chart Below).

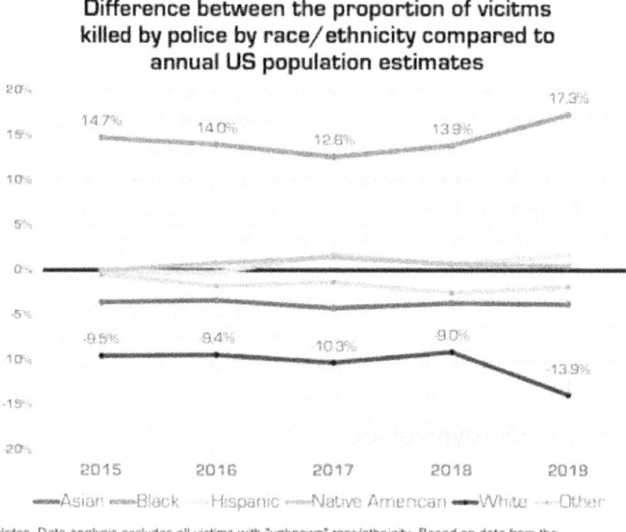

There might be many circumstances that yield the over-representation of blacks involved with lethal treatment by police in the United States as a whole. These circumstances take on a social context. It could be neighborhood segregation, income and wealth inequality, school resource inequality, white supremacy, systemic racism, poverty, racism, voter suppression, labor force discrimination, etc. These were some of the social issues that I mentioned earlier in this chapter.

Some incidents cause protests by Blacks. The Black Lives Matter movement focuses on the treatment and brutality of blacks by police, where lethal force is used mostly. These victims or suspects were unarmed during the time of the altercation with law enforcement. In 2015, 34 percent of whites unarmed were killed by cops compared to 40 percent of unarmed Blacks killed by the police. In 2018 whites' unarmed interaction with cops increases to 49 percent with Blacks unarmed decreased to 34 percent and Hispanics to under 15 percent. The data does show that whites make up a higher number of unarmed people being killed by police because they have a larger percentage of people in the general population.

The data on blacks being killed unarmed shows some discrepancies in the information relative to the United States population. The data also shows Whites and Hispanics underrepresented among the victims. (See Chart Below).

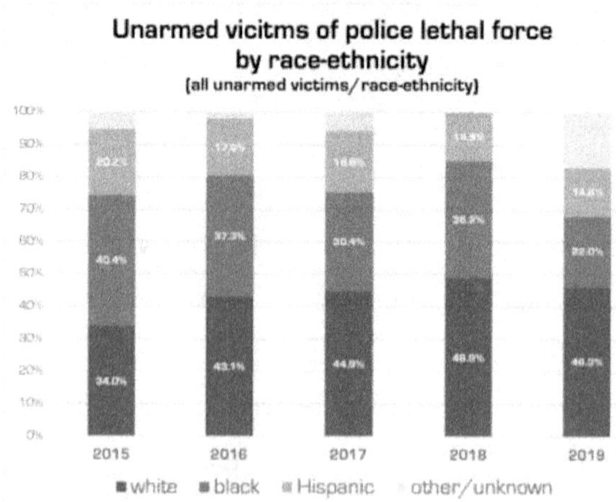

We have known that recently with the deaths of George Floyd, Breonna Taylor, Rayshard Brooks, Natosha "Tony" McDade, and Yassin Mohamed that Blacks are mostly killed by police. Blacks are disproportionately killed by the use of lethal force when they are unharmed by police relative to the general population. When you do examine deaths in 2019 of people killed unarmed by police, a similar proportion of whites, blacks, and Hispanics killed by police were unarmed when killed. I can't understand why these victims would pose life-threatening issues to armed cops unless they have a knife or some other kind of weapon that would be considered lethal? Why do some cops always have to shoot to kill instead of trying another mechanism to stop the victim from running away from the scene of an altercation with an armed cop? These are questions that we need to examine to see if we can come up with some rational answers.

The Black Lives Matter Movement has brought on an awareness of the treatment of Blacks by white police in areas where crime is a serious issue in society. Death seems to be a plague in some black communities in the United States. The effort of this movement (organizing, protesting, advocating, etc.) has opened the eyes of certain police departments in some predominantly black communities around the United States with an attempt to eliminate lethal force against unarmed citizens and especially people of color.

Some people feel that lethal force has become racially charged that seems to target more African American communities where the majority of cops in these communities are mostly white. These statistics do change every year.

Comments:

We have seen some tragedies in recent years where blacks continue to be killed unarmed by white cops. We have to examine different methods to be proactive when we are stopped by any cops. We can come up with ways to modify our behavior so that we will not trigger cops to kill us. This will be discussed later in the book. We can react differently when stopped by a cop and maybe this behavior will save our lives. The way that we conduct ourselves when arrested can determine our fate. We might be killed or live to see another day. When stopped by the cops, there are some choices that we might have to make to save our lives. We have to think faster and get ahead of the cops.

Blacks Incarcerated

It is a known fact that Blacks are incarcerated in prisons in the United States more than five times at the rate of whites and at ten times the rate in some states. There are racial disparities in imprisonment. The reason could stem from many things. The question is: Do Blacks commit more crimes than other ethnic groups? It does seem that Blacks are more likely to be stopped by the police. Do we involve ourselves in criminal activities that land us in jail and prison? The data has shown in previous years that Blacks have surpassed whites in United States prisons. The Bureau of Justice Statistics is now seeing a decline in the number of black prisoners in comparison to whites and other ethnic groups in the past decade.

As you look at the year 2017, federal and state prisons had about 475,900 prisoners who were black compared to 436,500 white prisoners which is a difference of 39,400 inmates in prison according to the United States Department of Justice. Ten years before 2017, there were 592,900 black prisoners and 499,800 white prisoners which is a difference of 93,100. The information was compiled for only inmates sentenced to more than a year in prison. We can see the decline in the black-white gap during the years of 2007 and 2017 that was driven by a 20 percent decrease in the number of black incarcerations that exceeded a 13 percent decrease in the number of white inmates.

You can see a narrowing gap between white and Hispanic prisoners between 2007 and 2017 because the number of Hispanic prisoners increased while white inmates decreased somewhat. The racial disparities and ethnic makeup in prisons continue to look differently in the country as a whole. Blacks still represent 12 percent of the United States population but have a higher rate of incarceration compared to whites and Hispanics which is 33 percent of people in prison. Whites are represented by 64 percent of the adult population and 30 percent of prisoners.

Hispanics are 16 percent of the adult population but represent 23 percent of the prison population. There are different ways that we can examine the racial and ethnic differences of the prison population. You can look at the number of prisoners per 1,000.00. What we are seeing when you look at Blacks, Hispanics and whites is a decline in imprisonment rates since 2007. Among blacks since 2007, we can see a 31 percent decline. We can see a 14 percent decline among whites incarcerated and a 25 percent decline in incarcerations amongst Hispanics.

Mass incarceration has caused an examination of some of the causes of blacks being incarcerated for many years. Measures have been initiated to reduce the incarceration of blacks in large numbers. Crime rates have been declining since the mid-1990s and some prison populations have been on the decline for some ethnic groups. We have seen some depopulation in New Jersey, New York, Rhode Island, and California declining by 20 to 30 percent. We wish that we could say that about other states in the Union. These states are bad for blacks because of crime in Wisconsin, Ohio, Michigan, Iowa, Mississippi, and Illinois.

Certain circumstances do cause racial disparities in incarceration. We have a high rate of black incarceration compared to a low incarceration rate of white incarceration. The highest rate of disparity in imprisonment seems to occur in the northeast or upper Midwest. Some Southern States seem to have lower ratios. States like Arkansas and Florida have both black/white ratios of imprisonment below the national average. These states still incarcerate African Americans at a higher percentage rate of disparity and a lower rate of disparity for whites that commit similar crimes.

Another explanation for racial disparities lies in the advantages and disadvantages of people of color before they encounter the criminal justice system. Blacks have to deal with so many social factors in African American Communities that are not prevalent in white communities. Other factors like poverty, unemployment, housing, and family differences affect the incarceration of blacks. Blacks live in poverty-stricken neighborhoods where they are vulnerable and susceptible to higher rates of crime. This would include more violent crime.

Structural disadvantage starts early in the black community for which blacks have no control. Some blacks are involved in juvenile crime and this eventually leads to more serious criminal offenses. Black Youth are more likely to have unstable family situations, exposure to community violence, gangs, higher rates of unemployment, and more school dropout. This is why reform is vital to every community. Reform has been a major issue for years to decrease the rates of incarceration of blacks and juvenile detention centers for juveniles. Some states like New Jersey have initiated positive reforms affecting the sentencing of blacks, drug-free school zone, and other measures for reform. New Jersey did experience an increase in incarceration from 1970 to the 1990s. In 2000, the state did see a decline in incarceration and reduced the prison population by 28 percent. In 2010, New Jersey reforms were passed to modify sentencing laws associated with drug-free zone laws. Other states have been working on initiatives to decrease the incarceration of blacks. Drugs did contribute to the higher incarceration of blacks and people of color.

Criminal Justice Reform has become an important aspect of dealing with some of the discrepancies of blacks being locked up for many years in the criminal justice system. Some states have been experiencing budget restraints when it comes to the Criminal Justice System and how it has affected the black population for decades. We have to deal with chronic racial disparities that engrain state prisons. Racial dynamics of incarceration have improved over years in the 2000s when we examine gender. During the years 2000 and 2009, incarceration rates for black females dropped 31 percent from 205 per 100,000 to 142 per 100,000. Still, not enough attention has been given to the chronic racial disparities of incarceration of blacks. The United States needs some serious sustainable reforms that are necessary to deconstruct the current system of mass incarceration that has had a profound impact on the Black community for decades.

Comments:

We all know that there need to be more reform initiatives to keep Blacks out of prison. Some states have made outstanding progress addressing the subject in a very serious manner.

Protests and Demonstrations

Please understand that there is nothing wrong with peaceful protests and demonstrations for a worthy cause. We have to believe that riots are very destructive and they do great harm to different cities in the United States. They create havoc and despair. People are killed in riots and we know that race riots stem from police brutality when blacks are the victims. A Black Lives Matter protester was shot in Austin, Texas in 2020 marching in downtown Austin. Police claimed that the protestor was armed with a weapon that placed people in danger.

In Portland, Oregon in 2020 a protest turned into a serious riot because of the behavior of some of the participants. These protestors jumped over fences that were protecting certain areas of the city near the Courthouse in downtown Portland. We also knew that Federal agents will irritate protestors and this escalated into violence and unnecessary treatment by law enforcement.

Protests can last for long periods and this has such an insightful effect on certain cities in the United States. The Protest in Portland, Oregon lasted fifty-nine days. During this period President Trump decided to intervene by sending Federal agents to restore peace in cities. Most of the governors in these cities didn't want any assistance from the Federal Government because they felt that their cities didn't want to be in charge of controlling any of the violence that struck their cities.

A riot started in Eugene, Oregon in 2020 when protestors for the Black Lives Matter movement were protesting in solidarity with other groups stating that "All Lives Matter", according to the police. Police were trying to stop the vandalism of businesses. Protestors were also throwing rocks at police escalating the violence. People were arrested because of their behavior. Peaceful protests evolved in Oakland, California in 2020 by marching in the streets to support the "Black Lives Matter" movement by supporting the protests in Oregon.

There were some agitators according to the Oakland Police Department, among 700 demonstrators, who led to vandalism by breaking windows, spray painting walls, and releasing fireworks. Some of the protests caused some serious fires.

There were protests in Seattle as well. This resulted in fifty-nine officers being hurt that clashed with protestors and forty-seven arrests were made. Some of the protests were peaceful until night came. The protestors became violent by throwing rocks and explosives at the police. An officer was hospitalized because of the destruction by some of the protestors. This protest also became very violent in Seattle when windows of cars and some businesses were broken into near downtown Seattle as protesters marched through the area.

We know that it is a known fact that some of these riots were initiated by the "Black Lives Matter" movement because of the killing of African Americans by police and because of the treatment of blacks during crime pursuits. Some Blacks and Whites have a low tolerance level when it comes to the treatment of Blacks during police encounters with law enforcement. Protests and riots have stemmed from the deaths of Breonna Taylor, George Floyd, and other blacks killed by police in 2020.

Comments:

There is nothing wrong with peaceful protests for issues that you strongly believe in. We all have the right to protest peacefully without any kind of violence and destruction of cities. Rioting is very destructive and destroys cities. Rioting has a financial impact on infrastructure of certain areas. People's lives are jeopardized by the result of rioting. Protests can be very effective in making a point.

The Impact of Looting

Looting is dangerous and very detrimental to any city. It disrupts a community and causes great harm and chaos to a given city. People's lives can be placed in great danger. It jeopardizes businesses in cities and creates financial suicide in a city or neighborhood. Destroying businesses that you depend upon in an area is beyond my comprehension as a sane person and an African

American in the United States. Why would you burn down the businesses that you rely on in a given area or city? Why would you burn down the only fast-food restaurant that you have in your neighborhood? Black and Whites loot but Blacks seem to do it more frequently because of their dismay of police behavior in murdering blacks in cities around the United States.

Thousands of people have gone to the streets in cities across America to protest institutional racism and police brutality because of the death of George Floyd, Elijah McClain, Philando Castile, Breonna Taylor, Michael Brown, and other African Americans killed by law enforcement along with Walter Wallace. People decided to break windows, burn down property that doesn't belong to them, and steal goods. Just because the police behave in an unethical manner or do something that you dislike or disagree with, this isn't a ticket to destroy a city. This kind of aggression has serious consequences and will send you to jail. The worst thing is creating a criminal record on top of paying large fines for breaking the law. You will wind up racking up expensive fines that you can't afford.

It is a proven fact that looters are only a small percentage of the demonstrations and protesters who are conducting themselves in an orderly fashion in a nonviolent or threatening manner.

The looting has almost become a disease in some American cities around the world. In lower Manhattan, people went on a rampage of stealing shoes and electronics. In 2020 in Minneapolis, looters almost cleaned out a Target store because of the death of George Floyd. This caused so much anger and rage in the city. As I watched what transpired on television, it was very disturbing and immoral from my point of view. It was disappointing to see that most of the looters were Black which has been a perception of white people in society. There was violence taking place all over the world during the death of George Floyd. We saw people looting and destroying property in Grand Rapids, Michigan, and other cities in the United States. In some instances, there were also whites looting along with blacks.

People were angry, upset, outraged by the conduct of police officers killing blacks in cities. This has caused so much unrest in the world. This still doesn't give our people the right to go out and behave in a manner that will get them arrested and placed in jail. Everything has a process and if you follow the right protocol, you can change some things. Taking the law into your own hands can cause some serious problems and destroy the area where you depend on certain services in the community.

There are some different channels where we can express our disdain in society. We can express our frustration in a nonviolent way. We know that there is some unprovoked violence against black people and peaceful protesters. After the death of George Floyd in Minneapolis in 2020, it was appalling to see the behavior of blacks looting in Minneapolis because of the tension that was caused by the death of George Floyd. When someone is killed and we disagree with the results of shooting or killing, this doesn't give us the right to steal and take personal property in our neighborhood through stealing and other unethical behavior that should never be tolerated by any race especially Blacks. People had broken into a Target and were walking away with a large basket of stolen items for retaliation for the killing of George Floyd.

The looting caused a change reaction in some black communities around the world.

Mayor Lightfoot in Chicago didn't think that her looting was a result of what happened in Minneapolis after the death of George Floyd. She said that it stemmed from a police shooting in Englewood earlier in the day. Regardless of what the looting stemmed from; it shouldn't have ever happened. This is one of the main reasons that so many stereotypes are created about Blacks and their conduct as the ringleaders when people attach these stereotypes to our people. When you take resources from your community, this has such a very negative impact on the community serving other people.

Comments:

I have never been against nonviolent protests. Looting is something that I despise no matter what the circumstances are. It destroys the livelihood of a city. It isn't right to take things that don't belong to you. It isn't a ticket to obtain things that you didn't pay for. Looting isn't worth developing a police record that might stay with you for the rest of your life. It brings hardships to cities.

The Incarceration of Black Women

When I had started writing this book, I never thought I would be covering the topic of incarceration of black women and the impact that it has had in the black community. It is alarming when you look at this topic in comparison to the black that have high incarceration statistics. There are some behaviors that wind up changing the dynamics of a human being and they are situated in circumstances that lead to their incarceration. Some black women can be categorized as being tough and mean. All people that have a tendency to exert anger don't commit crimes in America.

There are some women whom I have known to have been involved in crime but it is kind of rare to know a substantial number of black women who might go to prison or end up in jail for breaking the law. Television did a special on black women who were serving jail time for minor infractions and not paying fines and some of the fines were so small and it was disturbing to see that these women were in jail. This one community created a fundraiser to raise money for women who were in jail for not serious crimes and misdemeanors. Black women seem to be incarcerated disproportionately compared to other ethnic groups. This is why they have high incarceration rates similar to black males committing some of the same crimes.

Infant mortality is having a very negative effect on women of color along with mass incarceration. These are some major issues in the black community in 2021 and beyond. These issues are dealt with on separate tracks having structural racism connecting these critical issues.

Structural racism creates stress for black women when they come into contact with the justice system that destroys their health and the health of their children. It is a fact that today, infants born to black mothers die at twice the rate of those children born to white mothers. This terrible disparity cannot be fully explained by differences in income, education, or even health care; the data indicates that cumulative stress from generations of structural racism is driving this epidemic. To acknowledge this persistent problem, lawmakers must examine structural racism in all its forms focusing on mass incarceration of black women.

When we think of structural racism, it is defined as a system of public policies, institutional practices, cultural representation, and other issues that work in reinforcing methods to perpetuate racial inequality against women of color. The criminal justice system is probably the clearest example of structural racism in America. America has the highest incarceration rate in the world, and an exhaustive burden of contact with the system has definitely fallen on communities of color, targeting African Americans. As I indicated in other chapters of this book, African American adults are five times more likely to be incarcerated than white Americans. According to certain data, African Americans are twice as likely as their white counterparts to have a family member or relative imprisoned at some point during their childhood. Viewing incarceration rates more than 500 percent higher than they were forty years ago, the black Millennials and other post-Millennials are at a higher risk of contact with the system than any previous generation. In 2018, a new CAP analysis found that one in four black Millennials had an incarcerated loved one before they turned eighteen years of age. As you examine those born in the early 1990s, the rate is almost one in three.

Mass incarceration has caused some long-term physiological effects that have caused a range of health issues, including mental disorders, diabetes, asthma, hypertension, HIV, and Hepatitis C. We know that mass incarceration can also directly and indirectly affect infant mortality. The direct effects are well-documented, its indirect effects are pervasive and damaging but largely overlooked. Individuals that are incarcerated can face increased risk of sexual violence and infectious diseases. They lose contact with family and friends; as well as trauma resulting from harsh prison policies and practices. The incarceration of a loved one or breadwinner when it is the mother can cause families and friends a substantial amount of emotional distress, loss of income and property, and residential instability. These issues create a higher risk of post-traumatic stress disorder (PTSD), anxiety and can lead to serious depression.

The Center For American Progress believes that toxic stress from experiences with the criminal justice system has contributed to the disparity in rates of black and white infant mortality. Experts have estimated that infant mortality rates today would be 7.8 percent lower and that disparities between black and white women would be 15 percent smaller if incarceration rates had remained at 1970s' levels. Major interventions are necessary today to close the gap and bring the United States up to par with other developed countries.

This article has focused on the analysis of the Center For American Progress analysis and summaries of existing research to detail the effects of mass incarceration on black women and children. They have discussed how black women's extreme contact with the criminal justice leads to increased stress and disparities in health and infant mortality. In some analyses, some data is limited when structural racism is examined.

Structural racism demonstrates how countless women and children deal with harmful stressors associated with the criminal justice system. The number of women incarcerated increased dramatically in recent decades from just 26,000 in 1980 to 219,000 in 2017 and has gone up in 2019. The spike in black female incarceration has disproportionately affected women of color, especially young black women. According to CAP, black women overall are twice as likely to be imprisoned than their white counterparts. If black women incarcerations continue to rise beyond 2022, black women ages eighteen to nineteen are three times more likely to be imprisoned than white women and other ethnic groups. This also means that if incarceration trends continue beyond 2022, one in eighteen black women will be incarcerated at some point in their lifetime.

It is still a terrible scenario to think that black women and their families, especially within younger generations, are also more likely than their white counterparts to have some contact indirectly with the criminal justice system through the incarceration of a household member.

As the Center for American Progress examines the data from nine states, African American children across generations have had more than twice the odds of having someone in their household incarcerated as compared to white children.

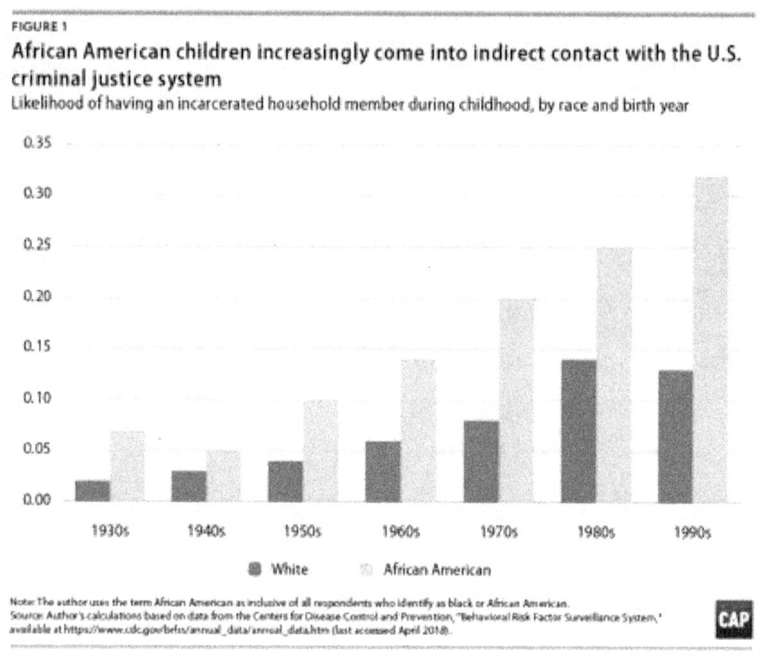
FIGURE 1
African American children increasingly come into indirect contact with the U.S. criminal justice system
Likelihood of having an incarcerated household member during childhood, by race and birth year
0.35
0.30
0.25
0.20
0.15
0.10
0.05
0.00
1930s
1940s
1950s
1960s
1970s
1980s
1990s
White
African American
Note: The author uses the term African American as inclusive of all respondents who identify as black or African American.
Source: Author's calculations based on data from the Centers for Disease Control and Prevention, "Behavioral Risk Factor Surveillance System,"
CAP

This is very true even after controlling for income level; geography; and family history of addiction, mental illness and some kind of abuse in the family dynamics. The data also show that younger generations are at a greater risk with 27.4 percent of black Millennials having indirect contact during childhood, compared to 10.7 percent of Baby Boomers. CAP data also found that racial disparities in indirect contact with the criminal justice system will persist long after childhood. It has been determined that one in four African American baby boomers—26.4 percent report having some family member incarcerated at some point in their lifetime, compared with just 15.1 percent of white Baby Boomers. When you look at other disparities, even after controlling for other important variables such as income and education, they contribute to women being incarcerated. As the Millennials and post-Millennials are coming of age during this period of incarceration, they are more than likely to report higher rates of contact with the criminal system during their lifetimes.

There have been millions of women exposed to the harmful effects of mass incarceration during their lifetimes. They could have experienced imprisonment personally or they have an incarcerated loved one, the contact with the criminal justice system causes severe anxiety and stress that destroys and undermines the long-term health of so many black women who have been imprisoned for long periods of time. Any kind of affiliation with the criminal justice system that involves crime and imprisonment is detrimental to everyone's mental stability and welfare.

We know that contact with the criminal justice system is so stressful no matter one's economic status, race, gender, or age. Important groups like SisterSong Women of Color Reproductive Justice Collective and the Center for Reproductive Rights have highlighted, many women—especially black women—are exposed to stressors when they are incarcerated. The data illustrates that 86 percent of incarcerated women are survivors of past sexual violence, but they still are subject to procedures that fail to consider past trauma.

These procedures have included cavity searches, pat-downs, and shackling. It is a known fact that most jails and prisons lack adequate mental health services, menstrual hygiene products, or gynecological and obstetric care—maintaining the stress and trauma experienced while incarcerated.

It is a sad scenario in some prisons and jails is that the majority of incarcerated women are also mothers—mostly to young children. Before their incarceration, most of these women were the primary caretakers of their children. This seems to be more prevalent in so many black women's homes. There are a lot of single-parent homes in some black communities as I stated in another chapter. Some of the facilities where women are confined are located more than 100 miles from their families, and more than one-third (38 percent) will not see their children even once while incarcerated. When mothers lose contact with their children this increases their stress levels among incarcerated mothers. The situation is worse when many siblings are split up when a mother is separated from her children. When this happens, incarcerated mothers are four times more likely to experience high levels of maternal strain or significant stress from feeling like they are not fulfilling their obligations as a mother. When children are placed in foster care, incarcerated mothers risk never getting their children back, even when they have demonstrated the ability to care for them upon their release from jail or prison. This has been known to cause depression for black mothers than the general population.

The U.S. Bureau of Justice Statistics, states that 4 percent of women in federal prison and 3 percent of women in state are pregnant at the time of their incarceration. For some of these women, negligent correctional procedures can produce many levels of stress and add to pregnancy-related mental health disorders, which are already disproportionately experienced by black women. Looking back in 2010, the most recent year for which aggregated data are available, dozens of states did not require medical examinations or prenatal nutrition counseling for pregnant inmates. These states failed to offer pregnant women the proper guidance on recommended activity levels or safety measures during pregnancy. The state also limits the shackling of pregnant women—including during the transportation to the doctor and to the hospital for labor, delivery, and recuperation. Banned by the Federal Bureau of Prisons in 2008, this cruel method increases the stress level of women and jeopardizes birth outcomes. When incarcerated women give birth, they are frequently rushed back to prison and are unable to breastfeed their babies like mothers that are not incarcerated or otherwise care for and bond with their newborns.

This traumatic experience can produce mental and physical scars that destroy the long-term health and well-being of women and their infants. As I indicated earlier, black women are overrepresented in the criminal justice system and this creates an abundance of stress and other mental issues. This reality adds to health disparities between African American women and white women.

Some Factors That Have Contributed to Incarceration of Black Women

Policies have been implemented under the so-called tough-on-crime, war on drugs, and "Broken Windows" approaches to policing contributed to an explosion in the United States prison population. It is a known fact that one in three Americans carries the stress of a criminal record, and nearly half of American children have a parent with a criminal record. It does seem like more black children have more parents with criminal records compared to other ethnic groups especially white Americans. This causes African Americans with criminal records to suffer severely lifelong consequences, such as barriers to housing, education, and employment, among others. When you look at the years 1980 and 2014, the population of women who were incarcerated grew 700 percent.

As you examine the policies below, they have a disproportionate impact on women of color. Listed below are six things that all Americans should know about black women and the criminal justice system:

African American women are more likely than women of other races to go to prison during their lifetimes. According to a 2003 Bureau of Justice Statistics special report, one in every eighteen African American women will go to prison during their lifetime if incarceration rates continue at the same rate. This is far greater than the rates for white women and Latinas—one in 111 women and one in forty-five women, respectively.

African American women are significantly overrepresented in state and federal prison populations. According to a 2014 Bureau of Justice Statistics report, the incarceration rate of African American women was more than double the incarceration of white women. More specifically, 109 out of every 100,000 African

American women in the United States were sentenced to state or federal prison by the end of 2014, compared with fifty-three out of every 100,000 white women.

The war on drugs has negatively affected women of color. Women are more likely to be incarcerated for drug offense. Furthermore, research has shown that although all women use and sell drugs at the same rate, women of color—particularly African American women and Latinas—have a higher likelihood of becoming involved in the criminal justice system for a drug offense. Generally, women involved in the drug trade have scant knowledge of actual drug dealing operations, which gives them little leverage in negotiating shorter sentences.

Incarcerated women are likely to be victims of abuse, have a history of substance abuse, and/or suffer from mental health issues. A 2007 study found that nearly all incarcerated women have experienced a "traumatic event"—with 71 percent reporting that they were "exposed to domestic violence." According to a 2008 study, 73 percent of women in state prisons and 47 percent of women in federal prisons used drugs prior to going to prison. Additionally, approximately 73 percent of women in state prisons and 75 percent of women in local jails have signs of mental health disorders, compared with only 12 percent of women in the general U.S. population.

Approximately 12,000 pregnant women, or approximately 6 percent of incarcerated women, are incarcerated each year. Many of these women are subjected to the dehumanizing and dangerous practice of shackling during childbirth. This practice is not only dangerous to the mother—limiting her mobility to manage the pain of childbirth—but it also puts the child at risk, reducing physicians' ability to safely deliver the baby. Unfortunately, twenty-eight states have no laws prohibiting the practice.

African American and American Indian girls have higher rates of placement in juvenile residential detention facilities than those of other racial and/or ethnic groups. African American girls are also more likely than other girls to face suspension. African American and American Indian female juveniles were placed in residential detention facilities at rates—1.7 times and more than four times, respectively—higher than their non-Hispanic white counterparts. Additionally, African American and American Indian female juveniles were placed in these facilities at rates of 113 per every 100,000 girls and 167 per every 100,000 girls, respectively, while non-Hispanic white female juveniles were held in these facilities at a rate of 35 per every 100,000 girls.

We have a broken criminal justice system that has affected all Americans, particularly women and men of color. The rates of black women and black men are just staggering in comparison to whites. Women are the fastest-growing portion of the United States prison population, and data show that women of color continue to be incarcerated disproportionately in the criminal justice system. We cannot reiterate the importance and how essential it is to implement reform that affects black women and men more positively. Reform is a vital function of moving forward by assisting black women and men with reforms that are going to have a positive effect in the criminal justice system. Criminal justice reform is also essential to make sure that these women have the opportunity to succeed in society once they have paid their debts to society.

Chapter Three

Closing the Achievement Gap of Blacks in Education

Understanding the role of culture in development is important. My first jobs exposed me to people who saw the world differently than I. The more I learned about why they held their beliefs, the more I understood. Today, I ask my teacher education students to think about their own cultures and life experiences as the first step in understanding and relating to the children and families they will encounter in the field.

***Barbara T. Bowman

My mother, who had less than two years of formal education, once asked me what I do for a living. I told her I try to incorporate a rich diversity of experiences for kids into educational settings. She said "Why that's just common sense! They pay for that?" Common sense, and still it's an uncommon practice among many.

*****James P. Comer**

We must acknowledge the broader diversity in and of the African American experience and celebrate that all Black children are born geniuses. Black students continue to pursue educational excellence despite the many unnecessary obstacles they face due to constructions and perceptions of race, class, gender, and sexual orientations in America.

******David J. Johns**

People continue to comment that early childhood education is vital to the educational journey of a child. It has become increasingly important in the last decades. It is an especially important aspect of American life and the life of African Americans. The outcomes can be incredibly positive at the early stages of a child's life. School performance has been an issue for African Americans. The literature states that educational achievement between African Americans and other groups is overwhelming and disheartening. It appears that African American children, on average, continue to score lower on tests and are given lower grades than Asian, White, and Latino students. Many of them fail courses and drop out of school. Other Blacks progress through school but do not excel; some of them enroll less in honor courses in high school or are accepted into competitive four-year colleges. When I was teaching in 2016, I was in the media center and the high school where I worked was recruiting students for an Honor's English Class. I sat and waited cautiously to see who would show up. This school system had about a 30 percent black student body. I wanted some black students to sign up for this class. There was not one student that showed up for this class. This was very disappointing because I had my hopes up. To my dismay, this was a sad day at the high school. In all honesty, I was under the impression that this teacher did not want any African American students to sign up. I might be wrong with my interpretation of that situation. As this white instructor talked to the students, he went over some extremely strict rules. Discipline might have been one of the reasons that he didn't want any blacks in his class.

The achievement gap has always haunted black students and their communities. This is a problem that affects the well-being of the country. Researchers conclude that the educational achievement gap is a crisis in America, and it imposes on the United States, the economic equivalent of a permanent national recession. It was stated in some of the other chapters that past and present economic and social conditions are at the top of the list as the root of the achievement gap issue. The efforts to eliminate and destroy the ill effects of prejudice and discrimination for African Americans have not been effective enough and this is why we continue to experience inequities in almost every aspect of life, especially in education. So many technological changes have decreased the educational requirements for successful, fulfilling careers, placing a greater strain on underserved communities and black schools.

Understanding these factors, teachers will be able to develop and administer the strategies needed to address school failure that leads to success by increasing more opportunities for life success for more African American students. There are also other children from other communities of color that become victims of racism and poverty too. Some of these groups have their unique history of dealing with oppression because they also share the same challenges and issues. It is vital to understand the differences and similarities among groups. This makes teachers learn the strengths of children and families when designing programs that address their educational and developmental needs. When teachers aren't reaching certain students in different grades, this is a red flag for that school system and should be addressed immediately. There is no doubt that African children are born with the ability to learn but some require different experiences to bring their potential to the surface and to fruition. It is a known fact that students develop some capabilities through their interactions with people and things that encourage the brain circuitry controlling children's physical, social, emotional, and cognitive skills. Some development is initiated by learning language, being sociable, using symbols, and making categories. All children seem to master these skills at the same age in similar ways.

Some learning is related to the culture such as learning a new language, creating unique ways to categorize the environment, and interpreting the meanings of events. The vast majority of children learn a language (an inborn drive) but whether they learn Black English or Standard English depends on their life experiences in their communities. The development of language reflects individual and human biological potential, but it also reflects the linguistic characteristics of a particular cultural community. The social world of the family and the community plays an especially important role in how successful children will be in school. Adults must provide consistent physical care, social guidance, intellectual stimulation, and a lot of emotional support. Children attach themselves to great caregivers and come to depend on them for physical and emotional security growing up. They can identify with the intimate and begin to internalize the values, attitudes, ways of expressing themselves, approaches to solving problems of the caregivers. This creates a stage for social, emotional, physical, and cognitive characteristics that could be greatly beneficial to the child one day.

African American children who begin their lives in safe environments and have positive adult relationships seem to achieve their basic developmental potential. At the appropriate ages, African American children master the difficulties of language, process sensory information, manage their bodies, and even use symbols (such as a wooden block to represent a piece of toast). Some aren't exposed to a learning environment that entails opportunities to develop school-related language, knowledge, and skills such as literacy in Standard English, mathematics, or science. As they experience racial exclusion, they do not think the work of education will benefit them. We also have realized that some of them are growing up in circumstances that are too stressful for healthy development. These students are neglected from getting extra doses of emotional stability and direction needed to face adversity they have been exposed to, including the challenging demands of school.

It is very apparent that African Americans continue to experience the systemic challenges of poverty and racism in African American homes and African American parents continue to deal with these issues. So many experience self-doubt and powerlessness, others deny their culture and language to avoid rejection, ridicule, and others respond with rage and resentment as I stated in another chapter.

The Burden of Poverty

There has never been a question about the impact that poverty has had on the African American Community. Poverty places a huge impact and burden on families and a large number of African Americans live at an economic level that stresses families physically and mentally, with hunger, mental and physical illness, and despair being more frequent catastrophes that have a profound impact on education. It has been determined that poverty among African Americans exceeds that of any other group. We also know that poverty has declined for White, Hispanic, and Asian families in recent years, it has not for African Americans.

In 2015, some 38 percent of Black children lived below the poverty line—a percentage four times greater than that of White or Asian children. It is a travesty that families that are still struggling to make ends meet are more likely to be stressed and to have less time for their children than those from more economically advantaged groups. Also, children from poor and also less-poor African American families tend to reside in segregated, underserved neighborhoods, thus concentrating and reinforcing poverty's effects. As a consequence, generations of families and communities have been unable to provide the basic material resources their children require or protect children from the social and emotional stress of racism, poverty, and under-resourced environments. Poverty is a contagious disease that drains the social and emotional energy of families making it difficult for parents to respond with constructive intervention to typical childhood behavior, such as aggressiveness or impulsivity.

Some families and communities have adjusted to the harsh realities they face with aggression. And some children have learned to deal with problems by fighting rather than negotiating or working things out—behavior considered unacceptable in school, especially when teachers and administrators do not understand the roots of the behavior and do not help the children learn new behaviors in a warm, caring, culturally competent way. We made an adjustment to being on welfare for years and it just seems to be a natural thing. My mother seemed very comfortable receiving her food stamps and money allotment each month.

Toxic stress has been a major component of poverty. This includes exposure to extremes of violence and neglect, inconsistent and unreliable care, and unloving adults can be so stressful for children and their developmental potential is compromised or distorted. The results of such exposure can range from stunted emotional and intellectual development to death. The longer children live in a toxic environment, the more difficult and expensive it is to help them return to more typical developmental and learning trajectories. It is terrible that too many African American children live in toxic environments. Given this, it is a testament to African American families that despite the challenges that they face, so many find the resources to help their children avoid more serious developmental and learning problems. However, early recognition of support for children being affected by a toxic environment is essential if children are to avoid the pitfall of failed developmental and compromised future; exposure to severe neglect and abuse is increasingly difficult to treat. Timely family counseling and treatment, supportive alternative caregivers (often a grandparent or sitter), understanding teachers, supportive friends and neighbors, and/or therapeutic intervention can play a role in reducing stress and stabilizing children's development.

Culture is what groups create over time to adapt to their environment; it determines to a large extent how adults interact with children. Throughout the world, as parents adapt to different environmental challenges, they develop different child-rearing strategies, many of which are misunderstood by those unfamiliar with a community's history. For instance, as a result of transatlantic enslavement, Black people mixed the remnants of their home languages with English to create a dialect, or patrols, to communicate with one another (since they did not share a common language). The remnants continue today as Black English. The public impression, however, which has been used to justify abuse and injustice, is that this adaptive language, this dialect, is bad or broken English. Among that limited knowledge of Black Culture and linguistics, Black English is mistakenly assumed to be a product of ignorance than a creative form of verbal communication as complex Standard English.

Other behaviors which were fashioned to help African Americans cope with the dangers of slavery continue today because life is still perceived as dangerous. For instance, African

American children are often criticized for passivity, limited oral responsiveness, and disengagement. So many black parents teach this behavior as the best way for children to be safe in a hostile world.

The Challenges of School

The literature and data support that most African Americans do provide wonderful experiences for health, growth, and development considering some of the unbearable circumstances that have plagued them for decades. The question that seems to surface is why many African Americans have trouble learning in school. Could it be the different expectations for children between home and school? It might be that the skills and knowledge children gain at home and in their communities do not match the demands in school.

Children who learn Black English at home in comparison to Standard English seem to experience a steeper learning curve for school reading and writing (because Standard English is remarkably similar to academic English). When Black children live in low-income families in highly segregated communities, there is more likely to be a poor fit between their language experiences and what is required in school. This becomes a roadblock to school learning unless it is addressed early in life. Some students come to school who do not have the academic and social knowledge that teachers expect. They can deliver the names of things, ideas, people, and places that are meaningful to them but might know letter names or how to hold a book or what a farm is, or how to count to twenty. When this occurs, they might be labeled as developmentally challenged or having the limited potential to learn.

Another disadvantage that African Americans might have is limited vocabulary that could be a linguistic problem which could mean that the child is likely to have trouble with listening and comprehension in the early grades, especially when teachers read aloud complicated text that uses Standard and academic English vocabulary. Struggling with reading may also become a challenge which might lead to misbehaving and lack of motivation to try, coupled with embarrassment amongst peers in the classroom.

When Standard English is a challenge for children at home, curtailed with the stresses of growing up in isolated or under-resourced communities, even attending preschool may not suffice. Children may need meaningful relationships with teachers who believe they can learn, whom they want to please. Students need carefully structured curricula that expand across all grade levels so that children have the necessary tools to be successful in school. They also need teachers who direct them, coach them in how to get their needs met in school, how to ask for help, and how to accept it. When I was a media specialist teaching research skills in the media center, I could always tell the students that needed help because some of the other kids would finish ahead of them when they were assigned activities. There is nothing wrong with asking questions, and as I said earlier, some students fear asking questions even before a given assignment. Teachers must work extremely hard to make sure that all students are successful in the classroom especially people of color even if they need remedial assistance in the classroom.

Training for Teachers

It is essential to narrow the achievement gap for African American students and Special Needs children and this would include kids that are categorized to be in Special Education. There needs to be continued development for administrators, teachers, and support staff for ongoing professional development that enables them to zero in, pinpoint, and address so many issues that are affecting African Americans in the classroom. Their issues must be addressed coherently. When students are successful, the entire community is successful as well. When teachers apply effective engagement methods, African American children can experience the same academic and social development in school as white students. Preparatory institutions and professional development programs must prepare educators to understand the dynamics in which child development and academic learning are inextricably linked and they can facilitate learning from different cultural backgrounds. I can recall so many professional development workshops that addressed some of the needs in our district. Teachers can take what they have learned during professional development days and apply them in the classroom.

Recommendations for Eliminating the Achievement Gap for African Americans

These are recommendations by the authors of this article cited at the bottom of this page. Once we continue to follow and act upon the research with intervention while embracing a new understanding and accepting the discomfort of change, things will continue to improve for African American students. We will see long-term change when political, social, and even structural interests are engaged in the status quo. The change will occur the more we address a culturally appropriate asset-based understanding of our culturally-based children and families that we serve in education. This will require educators, administrators, and policymakers who:

- Know that today education is needed for the U.S. economy and the future of American democracy
- Understand the economic, political, and social contexts of families and recognize the complex interactions between all these and children's learning in school
- Appreciate that education begins before birth and that preschool education is essential as K-12 for all children at risk for school failure
- Understand that good education is far more than good test scores (all these are important); physical and mental health, the arts and music, citizenship, responsibilities, and empathic relationships are equally important and is planned and supported in school
- See the importance of facilitating engagement and learning for children from non-white backgrounds; integrating a positive racial identity with development, and of understanding teaching and learning as intellectually stimulating and culturally affirming experiences
- Plan for the prevention of difficult behavior and the promotion of responsible and effective family support to reduce costly generation-to-generation transmission of unrewarding behavior

- Work to foster authentic, reciprocal partnerships between families, children, teachers, and schools, in which the achievement of all students is encouraged and supported at home and school
- Select curricula and use teaching practices that are developmentally and culturally appropriate and thus are based on children's needs (rather than one size fits)
- Ensure that all children are given opportunities to develop an identity of excellence and scholarship that counters negative stereotypes
- Recognize cultural differences and set high expectations for all children to learn

It is strongly believed that a program carried out by people and organizations with a deep understanding of the complexities and the collaboration needed to support child development, who recognize the importance of education-both what is taught and how it is taught-and who focus resources to support family functioning will help close the achievement gap, benefiting our children, families, economy, and democracy in the long run.

College Education Disparities of Blacks and Latinos

As we continue to read and address some of the major issues in the black community, it is important to look at some of the inequalities in a college education. This is a major issue when it comes to obtaining a decent living and making good salaries as compared to whites. We have seen so many disparities throughout the book and there are racial disparities among college completers and a neglected college race gap.

Equity has been on the minds of people of color for decades especially in higher education which has focused on the serious gaps in access for black and Hispanic people. The awareness has been growing that going to college is sufficient and we know that luck hasn't always been in the hands of black students that might not graduate from college.

We know that there are some serious equities among students that have completed their college degrees. When you examine the federal data on the type of credentials students earn and the majors they study, you can see that blacks compared with white students, black and Hispanic graduates are far likely to have gone to for-profit colleges and less likely to have attended four-year public or nonprofit institutions. Blacks seem to attend institutions that have less money to spend on offering quality education. They are remarkably underrepresented in vital fields such as engineering and education, mathematics and statistics, and the physical sciences.

It would be wonderful if U.S. colleges and universities could eliminate these gaps among their graduates along, not considering disparities among those who don't proceed to graduation—a large number of students would have a different credential. The federal data on the number of degrees and certificates earned by black, Hispanic, and white students from 2013 through 2015 demonstrates that black and Hispanic graduates earned each degree type at the same rate as their white peers, more than one million more would have earned a bachelor's degree in just those three years.

These gaps also show up in the fields in which students obtain their bachelor's degrees. If Black and Hispanic bachelor's degree recipients were as likely to choose a career in engineering as white students, this country would have 20,000 more engineers from 2013 through 2015. The United States would have more than 30,000 more teachers of color if students of color were represented equally among education graduates.

As gender disparities are taken into consideration, inequalities are even starker. We know that white men earn bachelor's degrees in engineering at roughly six times the rate of Hispanic women and more than eleven times the rate of black women.

These unbelievable gaps show that true racial equity in higher education means more than attracting students to college and through college, it involves providing equality in the programs of study that are accessible and welcoming to them. As dramatic and surprising and entrenched as these gaps are, there are some positive steps that policymakers and researchers can take to offer more black students the opportunities that they deserve.

Researchers and institutions need to study more seriously the nature of the problem: Are students of color pursuing certain majors initially, only to switch later? Or are they steering clear of those fields entirely? Current state data systems that can track college outcomes by race will be beneficial to this research.

Institutions need to examine whether their pricing and advising practices are disproportionately pushing students into particular majors. Increasingly, colleges are charging different prices depending on the department in which students are taking classes. Evidence illustrates that these price differentials are disproportionately dissuading students of color from high-cost fields such as engineering. There is an obvious bias in the on-campus advising process could mean that black and Hispanic students are being dissuaded in certain fields while being encouraged to study in others.

Schools need to examine how introductory courses affect student persistence in each major. We need to ask are these courses designed to 'weed out" students that departments do not see as a good fit for the major? And if this is the case, does this harm underrepresented students of color. They surveyed 400 department chairs from top research universities revealed that respondents thought such a practice could be harmful to diversity.

There is a pure inequality where black students get their degrees and certificates. Acknowledging the racial differences in where students enroll, this isn't surprising. This gap is often overlooked. Blacks are more likely to receive their credential from for-profit and much less likely to receive their credential from a public four-year institution. Blacks' credentials are also more likely to come from schools that spend less money on their students, as well as schools with lower average SAT scores, lower faculty salaries, lower retention rates for first-year students, and higher student ratios.

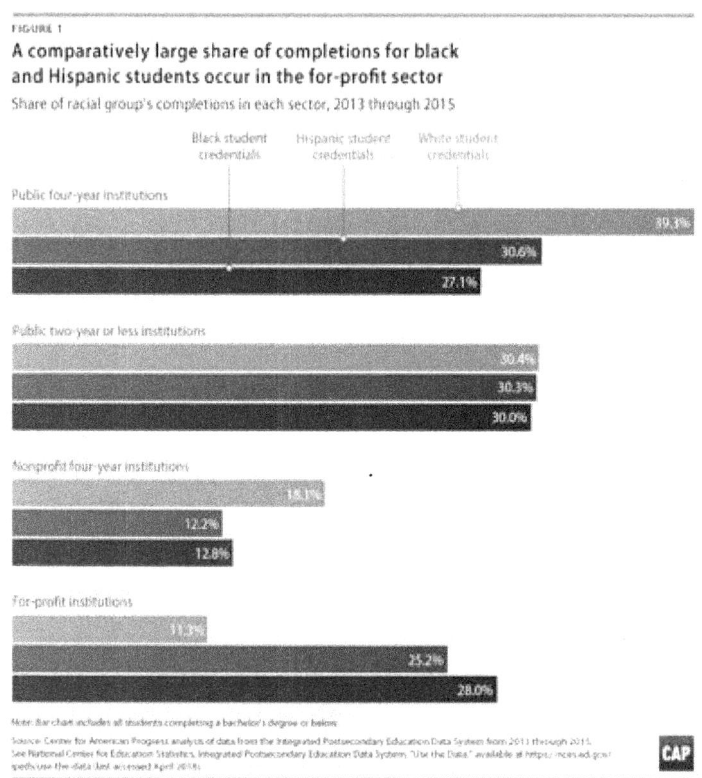

The study finds dramatic differences in the type of institution at which grades of different races complete their programs. As figure one shows, between 2013 and 2015, white students disproportionately earned their degrees or certificates at a public and non-profit four-year universities, while black and Hispanic completers were much more than likely to have graduated from for-profit schools. Giving the disturbing evidence that going to a for-profit college can be worse than not attending college at all, the comparative risk that black students receive their credentials from a for-profit college is perhaps the most concerning inequality uncovered in this analysis of disparities in colleges.

While 39 percent of the degrees and certificates white students receive come from public four-year schools, only around 30 percent of credentials awarded to black and Hispanic students are from public four-year colleges. A higher fraction of white students' credentials also come from private, non-profit four-year institutions.

In this case, the for-profit accounts for about 30 percent of black and Hispanic credentials, respectively, while making up just 11 percent of white credentials. To stress how extreme this difference is, consider that a larger share of credentials for black graduates comes from for-profit institutions than from public four-year schools. This, even though public four-year schools award twice as many credentials overall as for-profit schools.

Figure 1 also demonstrates that one of the higher education sectors in which white students and black and Hispanic students are equally represented is community colleges. Roughly 30 percent of each group graduates from public two-year schools. All told, if black and Hispanic graduates' credentials occurred in the sectors detailed in the chart above at the rate of white students, there would be roughly one million fewer credentials earned at for-profit institutions and over 600,000 more earned at public four-year schools.

Even if students of color earn credentials from institutions similar to those of their white peers attend, there can be inequities in how much an institution spends to educate their students. While higher spending levels do not necessarily guarantee the quality, recent research has established that increased spending has positive effects on both enrollment and completion for the affected students, which a 10 percent increase in spending changes the number of degrees awarded by 2 percent to 9 percent.

I was so glad that I decided to pursue my college dreams because I knew that I didn't want to have to depend on any kind of assistance program. Blacks have more opportunities to attend colleges and there is more funding and there are some colleges available. Blacks have ventured into black colleges and universities because they feel like the financial assistance is more abundant and they have more programs that can meet their needs as a student. I hate to discuss some of the disparities and how blacks have been steered in directions where they didn't feel comfortable because of their race. It just seems that we have obstacles to deal with in all aspects of society. I am so glad that I was very fortunate to have all the things that I needed while attending college in the early eighties.

Chapter Four

True Stories of Bad Behavior and Bad Choices

Overview: This probably was the most difficult chapter to write because I had relationships with all the people in the narratives and these people were very close to me because we grew up together and we did so many things together growing up in Gary. You will read a collection of different personalities. These people were singled out because I might have not liked them. That wasn't the case. I had no idea that they would make decisions that would impact the rest of their lives in such a negative tone. In a couple of the narratives, these individuals have passed on. For some strange reason, I never thought that I would be writing a book and that they would be subjects in the book. We all had a connection that was biological except for two of the characters in the narratives. Rosie wasn't a relative and her boyfriend wasn't a relative and the Postman and His Wife weren't related to me either. When you are growing up, you never think that bad things are going to happen to people that you love and care for.

In hindsight, I wanted everyone in the narratives to be successful, and being successful doesn't mean that they would have had to graduate from college. I had hoped that they all would have the possibility to retire in the same manner as I did. So many of our people were caught up in neighborhoods that were infested with drugs and this was an attraction for some of the high school students that lived in Gary. I would like to give you a small character analysis of the characters listed below. I don't think that their personalities contributed to them making some bad decisions because I thought that they all had some good character attributes that attracted others in the same manner that attracted me to them.

Dwayne

Dwayne seemed like a very happy child growing up in Gary. He participated in sports like basketball and played football in high school. He was very close to his friends in high school. He was in the Boy Scouts and he enjoyed being outdoors and hunting with his father when he was in elementary school. Math was one of his favorite subjects in high school and he did go on to college and studied Business Administration but dropped out after his three years in college. As I had said, he never married and had two children. He worked a couple of jobs but never held any job for too long. In school, he worked and held a job as a student. They had college-bound programs in high school and he found enjoyment participating in these programs.

Dwayne was the eighth child in our family. As I stated earlier, I had six brothers and two sisters. I honestly did think that my mother and father were doing a good job of raising the entire family considering that we were on welfare and my mother was involved with a married man. Dwayne seemed to be a very happy child and he was interested in gymnastics as a kid. He participated in different programs that sponsored these kinds of activities. He did finish high school and he graduated from high school in 1978.

There were a lot of secrets that Dwayne seemed to hide. We were aware of him smoking marijuana and I am sure that it was my brother Randall that introduced him to that drug during high school in the late seventies. Smoking pot seemed to be a normal thing because other kids were smoking pot in high school and selling pot. As I had mentioned in **Chapter One,** my mother allowed my brother to smoke marijuana in the house. I am sure that Dwayne smoked pot with his friends. I was under the notion that it was tolerated by some African American parents. I might have been wrong. My parents didn't do anything to deter my brothers from smoking it. They were never disciplined for smoking marijuana.

Dwayne finished high school and he went on to attend Indiana University to study Business Administration. By this time, we were unaware that he had got involved with smoking crack cocaine. We discovered this while he was attending Indiana University. He was able to pursue his studies even though he was addicted to crack cocaine which we found out before he dropped out of Indiana University in 1980. He managed to complete three years of college after being addicted to crack cocaine. It was amazing that he could stay focused on his academics at Indiana University. I thought he was really smart and he was always good in math. This was one of his strongest subjects in high school.

He had an incident where my father had given him money to pay for his classes at college as he was entering into his second year at Indiana University. He called my father and informed my father that the money that was given to him to pay for tuition was stolen by his roommate or some other person that lived in the dormitory. So, at that point, my father believed him and so did we. My father sent him the same amount of money that he had given to him previously for his classes. Not once did it ever occur to us that he might have used this money for drugs. We had no idea that he was addicted to crack cocaine.

After dropping out of Indiana University after three years of college, he moved back to Gary to live with his brothers and a sister that were still living in my mother's house in 1980. I had a sister that lived in the house as well. She had a very volatile relationship with Dwayne. They didn't like each other. Dwayne was living in the house without any responsibility of contributing to any of the household expenses. My brother (Allan) was on VA disability who carried all the expenses and provided food for all the people that lived in the house. Dwayne and my sister Mary got into serious altercations and she almost stabbed him with a knife. Dwayne just had a very nasty attitude about Mary. They didn't like each other even when my mother was living. Mary was an alcoholic at the time which caused their relationship to be volatile. There were times when I thought that she was going to stab him to death.

When my mother passed in 1981, I wanted to sell the house and give everyone a percentage of the money. One of my older brothers wanted to keep the house and allow Dwayne to stay there along with my other brothers and sister. Luckily, there was still some Homeowners' insurance on the house. The people that continued to live in my mother's house had to pay the utilities and pay the property taxes. They were in a good situation because the utilities were low on the property and the property taxes were reasonable. The property value of the home was less than $30,000. There was a renovation done on the home in the early seventies.

Dwayne lived in the house for years without contributing anything to the household or helping out with the utilities. I had told my older brother that wasn't living in the house that this wasn't fair to the other occupants in the house. I said why should Dwayne live in the house free of charge? Dwayne's main priority was always making sure that he had money to spend on crack cocaine. There were a couple of other people that lived in the house that agreed with me. While Dwayne was living in the house, there was a fire. I still to this very day don't know how the first fire started in the house. This was the very first fire to occur at the property. There was some speculation that the fire was started intentionally but this couldn't be proven. During this first fire, Dwayne wasn't a suspect. The insurance company honored the claim and provided a place for the residents to stay along with a $30,000 stipend for other expenses while the house was being renovated. Dwayne and my brother Marlon spent most of the insurance money foolishly with no receipts to show or any accountability for the money. There was no accountability as to how and where the insurance money was spent. Other brothers and sisters were inquiring about the money from the insurance.

My mother's home had another fire while Dwayne, Marlon, and Larry, and my sister were still residents in the home. The second fire was caused by Dwayne. Dwayne was dancing around the property with a gasoline can and my other brothers and sister said they watched him as he spilled the gasoline on the exterior part of the house. This was serious because while he was playing around with a gas can, the house did catch fire while my other siblings were in the house. They could have been seriously hurt by Dwayne's actions and his attempt to burn down the house. After the second fire, the people that lived in the house realized that Dwayne was seriously addicted to crack cocaine. He used the insurance money from the first fire claim to buy more drugs. That money assisted him with his continued drug abuse habit for a long time.

The people in the house decided to press charges against my brother Dwayne. He almost killed them by setting the house on fire while they were in the house. They knew that Dwayne had started the second fire. There was a trial and my other brothers and sister that were in the house during the fire were called to testify against Dwayne. My father also Dwayne's father (Malcolm) wanted the people that lived in the house to lie on the witness stand so that Dwayne wouldn't be charged. My brothers and sister said that they wouldn't perjury themselves on the witness stand. For some strange reason or another, Dwayne beat these charges and he wasn't charged with arson. I was appalled that my father would want my brothers and sisters to lie on the witness stand about a crime that they knew Dwayne had committed. Their lives were in jeopardy during the second fire. My father continued to support Dwayne after this serious crime. The insurance company honored the insurance claim again. I guess it was a good thing that the house still had insurance after two fires.

At that point, the people that still lived in my mother's house wanted Dwayne to move out of the house. That was a very hard task to achieve. Dwayne's drug use was out of control. My brothers had to keep their rooms locked when they weren't at the house. My brother Marlon had to always keep his room locked when he wasn't at the house. My brother Marlon had to keep his wallet locked in his car overnight. One brother informed me that while he was sleeping in his bed, he looked up at the ceiling in his room and Dwayne was dropping down in his room to steal his wallet. He was walking on the rafters where the installation was in the ceiling. This was how paranoid people had become about having Dwayne continue living in my mother's house. My brother didn't press any charges against him. Most of these incidents with Dwayne occurred around 1986.

My mother's house caught on fire three times. Everyone knew that Dwayne had started the last two fires but he was never charged. After the second fire, Dwayne gave away all the furniture and appliances, and beds in the house to neighbors. Luckily, they had insurance to replace these items. After the third fire that occurred at my childhood home, the insurance company denied the claim. We managed to sell the home and that was one way that Dwayne was finally removed from the home. Dwayne caused so much stress for my other brothers and sister that lived in my childhood home. We sold the home to Marshall Smith, a well-known realtor around 2009 in the Gary area. He was able to rent the home and make a small profit before the house was condemned and demolished. If you go and check out where the house stood on 2301 Palmer Street in Gary, Indiana, you will see a vacant lot without a house. It is very sad what happened to my childhood home and Dwayne is the blame for the demolishing and the destruction of my childhood home. Crack cocaine is a very dangerous drug and once you are addicted to it, it is very difficult to stop using it. Dwayne started smoking pot and eventually, the user wants something more powerful.

My older brother Clarence decided to go into business with two of his college buddies in the early seventies. They purchased a liquor store in Gary right across the street from the Gary Police Department. It was a thriving business in the early seventies. My mother would also work in the liquor store. She felt safe working at the store because it was right across the street from the police department. The mistake that my brother made was that he decided to allow Dwayne to become the manager of the liquor store when he dropped out of college. Clarence was never around the family during this time in history and he wasn't aware of Dwayne's drug addiction. Clarence was eventually bought out by his other two partners that helped him purchase the business. I am sure Clarence wouldn't have recommended Dwayne to become the manager if he would have known how severe Dwayne's drug use was. Eventually, my brother's partners

(Billy and Harold) would wind up closing the store because of terrible finances. Dwayne had stolen from the store to support his cocaine addiction. They lost everything and I still couldn't believe that Dwayne would be the cause of them losing their store because my brother was good friends with his former liquor store partners. How could Dwayne do something like this to my brother's friends when they trusted him to run their liquor store? These guys watched Dwayne grow up in Gary. Clarence had been friends with them for years. Dwayne was also running numbers out of the store. Clarence graduated with buddies that owned the liquor store.

Some behaviors are learned and some behaviors are acquired by the people you hang around and the company that you keep. Drug addicts find people that enjoy the same drugs that they enjoy. They have someone to continue down a path of illegal drug usage. They have a support mechanism that keeps them indulging in their drug usage. Once Dwayne dropped out of college, his life was never the same. He lost his ambition and desire to finish his college degree. Drug use became the staple of his trajectory. He continued to live to get high. He would do anything to keep his drug addiction going. He would steal from his friends and he kept trying to get that first intense high from crack cocaine. He continued to write bad checks and do other illegal things that might get him arrested or put in jail. His only goal in life was to keep his drug addiction going no matter what the consequences were. It is a shame that I would have to say that but it was the truth from my perspective and my other brothers and sisters would agree with my analogy and my interpretation of the situation that was going on at my mother's home.

After he dropped out of college, he did father two children and they are doing so much better than he is today. Luckily, they didn't get involved in drugs because they saw what it had done to their father, uncles, cousins, and other relatives. There was a time when I thought that my nephew was going down that path. He didn't have a good role model in Dwayne as a father in Gary. I can recall one time when I went over to my dad's house and my nephew Michael reeked of the smell of marijuana. I told him to come and talk to me in my father's basement. His eyes were red and he had a grin on his face. Pot changes the personality of some people. They seem more giddy than usual. I explained to him my unhappiness with him using pot in 2012. I told him that I was disappointed with him. He knew that I was upset with him because of situations that his father caused using drugs. I thought my nephew was better than that. I never had another conversation with him about using marijuana in the future. You can jeopardize your future and this can cause a whole lot of problems for you down the road especially when they started testing to see if people had marijuana in their blood until it was illegal. I have known people to take a blood test for drug users so that they would pass. I don't know how it was done but it was.

One mistake that my father made was allowing Dwayne to come and live with him around 2011 because his health was failing. He wanted someone to help him around the house and also assist with some of his finances. I couldn't stress enough to my father that he was making a big mistake allowing Dwayne to come and live with him. He had a bad experience with him when Dwayne lived with him before. My father started to notice that things started coming up missing around the house. My father started to question some things about Dwayne's conduct. My father told me that his money was missing out of his wallet. I had come to visit him on a Saturday along with my friend David because I paid all his bills once a month. My father was upset because he was wondering what had happened to his money. We all were trying to come up with an explanation about the situation. Dwayne said that his girlfriend was over to the house that night the money came up missing. Dwayne said that his girlfriend must have gone into my dad's bedroom and taken the money. David and I weren't buying that story. David said to me that Dwayne had stolen that money from my father. My father began to notice that whenever Dwayne would pay him for rent that the money that Dwayne had given him would come up missing. My father also said that he was sleeping one night and he noticed that Dwayne was crawling on the floor in his bedroom like a centipede. My father knew he was looking for his wallet to steal his money again. So, my father started to sleep with his wallet under his pillow. My father was eighty years old during that time when things started disappearing in his home.

My father was in denial about Dwayne's behavior for many years. He knew that Dwayne used marijuana regularly. He also knew that Dwayne used crack cocaine. Whenever Dwayne got into serious trouble, my father was always there to defend him even when he knew that Dwayne was wrong and committed a serious crime. If Dwayne was in jail, my father would bail him out. I can remember the time when Dwayne was hanging around with this woman he went to high school with. He only hung around her because he knew that she had crack cocaine and they would smoke it together. One day, Dwayne was over to her house the day that she received her welfare check. She had already cashed the check and he stole the money from her. This woman knew that Dwayne had stolen the money and at that time, she had another crack head at the house during the time the money came up missing. This crack head beat up Dwayne and forced him to return the money to the woman. Dwayne always needed to be bailed out of certain situations. He just seemed to be a magnet for attracting trouble and losers that had the same interests.

This woman called my father and told him that she was going to press charges against Dwayne for stealing her welfare money. She had about $300.00 in welfare money. She was going to use that to buy more crack. My father thought that she would press charges and he didn't want Dwayne going to jail. She persuaded my father to give her $300.00 so that she wouldn't press charges. What my father didn't know was that she had gotten her money back. He had given this woman money that she didn't lose. He was upset that this woman had scammed him because of what Dwayne had done. There are a lot of corrupt people in the world and this woman was one of them.

These are examples of how parents continue to defend their children when they know that what they have done is wrong. I can remember my father asking me for money to get Dwayne out of jail and I refused to give him any money. I told him if you want to get someone out of jail, you have to use your own money. I wasn't being mean-spirited but I wasn't going to waste money on someone for doing something that they shouldn't have been doing in the first place. Dwayne got into a lot of trouble and my father always came to his rescue no matter what the situation was believing Dwayne's side of the story. Dwayne couldn't do anything wrong in the sight of my father.

One of the most undesirable things in this world is when you can't trust your brother and other siblings because of their bad character. Dwayne has never done anything to help anyone. He even neglected his responsibilities of being a father. His entire life has always been about him in a very selfish manner. He could have done more for his children. The situation is terrible when you place drug use first instead of your children's welfare. He shirked his responsibilities as a father. I think he could have done more for his children.

When my father passed in 2014, I wanted Dwayne's son to move into the property. It was something that his son could afford and the utilities were not that expensive. My father moved into the Veteran's Facility in Gary before he passed. I knew that my father would never come back to his home. The plan was to allow Dwayne's son to move in and just pay the balance of the equity loan on the house. Before Dwayne's son could move in, Dwayne sold everything in the house. He sold things that his son needed to survive in the home. I would have pressed charges against Dwayne if I could have proved that Dwayne removed those things from the property. When Dwayne realized that my father wasn't going to return to his home, he and his girlfriend started clearing out the kitchen cabinets and boxing things to take to his girlfriend's house. I was the executor of my father's estate and I didn't give Dwayne or anyone permission to remove things from the property. I wanted to leave everything in the house for his son. Dwayne was still living in the house with my father. My father had some very nice things in the home before he was admitted to the Veteran's Facility. Things were missing in the house when we took my father to the facility. The snow-blower was missing and other valuable items in my father's garage were missing. My father had a very nice bicycle and that was missing.

My father had gotten to a point where he wanted Dwayne to move before he went to the Veteran's Home. We all were just frustrated dealing with Dwayne for many years. Some of the things that Dwayne did were just despicable and my father tolerated this conduct for years. My father and I went down to the Gary County Building to have Dwayne evicted. This was a difficult task. Once a person establishes residency somewhere, it is very hard to have them removed from the property. You have to go to court and get a lawyer. Dwayne refused to leave. This became a nightmare for my father. It is very difficult to have someone in your home and you have to watch their every move. You have to keep all your things locked up and secured so that they wouldn't be stolen. I told my father that if he would have listened to me years ago, he would have spared everyone and himself all the pain of dealing with Dwayne for so many years.

Dwayne's son was able to move into the property once my father was placed in the Veteran's Home. His son had to buy new furniture and other necessities for the home. Dwayne had broken up with his girlfriend where he had taken all the contents of my father's home. His girlfriend wound up keeping all of my father's possessions from the house. We never got any of the items back. We tried to retrieve some of the items taken from my father's home but we weren't that successful in getting most of the items back. We had other eggs to fry. The focus at that time was on my father.

Dwayne's life has been like a rollercoaster, it goes up and it comes down. He has been in rehab for the last twenty years without that much success. He hasn't been able to hold down a job. He has been homeless a couple of times. He continues to go in and out of rehab so that he has a place to live. Our family has done everything possible to help him with his drug addiction but each time, he falls back into the same conduct which makes it impossible for someone to help him. He lives in a small town in 2021 outside of Gary at a Mission. We don't know if he is still using drugs. We have spoken with him over the phone. It is hard to evaluate his present situation because we aren't around him enough. He was diagnosed with congestive heart failure in 2017 which runs in our family. He told me that he is on SSI. He is sixty years and has never owned a home in his entire life and that is very sad.

<u>Comments</u>: Telling this story has been very difficult for me because I always wanted my brother to take advantage of some of the opportunities that made me successful and some of my

other siblings. There are instances when the crowd that you hang around will have some impact on life and it could be negative or positive. He had some good role models with his older brother sisters. I am not giving up on Dwayne, I know there is still hope for him in life. I think that I heard that he has his apartment outside of Gary and out of the mission. That is the best news that I have heard in years.

Randall

Randall's life was about impressing his friends that he went to high school with. He was a very good dresser and had a taste for nice clothes. I think he was voted Best Dressed in high school. I know I would borrow his clothes in high school. Cleaning the family car and keeping it looking neat all the time was a full-time job for him because he wanted to drive his friends around town. Cigarettes became one of his pleasures when he was old enough to start smoking. I thought that he was a little mature when he was in high school because he seemed to do things that only adults did like drinking, smoking cigarettes and doing pot. He was the brother that brought marijuana into the home and got my brothers to start smoking the illegal drug when it was illegal. There were many character flaws that I found questionable. He seemed to only want to do things that benefit him. So many people in his class were heavy into drugs.

Randall was quite a character also. He was the sixth child in a family of nine. He was one of the five children that my mother had with my father, not her husband, Andrew. My father was Malcolm and my mother never married him. He was the married man my mother had a relationship with while she was still married to her husband, which is stated in **Chapter One.** I have made many references to him.

Randall introduced my other brothers to marijuana. He smoked marijuana regularly with his friends and people that lived in The Projects (West Park Manor) located next to our home. He seemed to only care about his friends than his brothers and sisters. He loved his friends. Some of us were in middle school and we didn't have a driver's license so if we wanted to go somewhere, we would have to depend on Randall. He never wanted to take us anywhere. We had to go and ask our mother and she would make him take us where we wanted to go. There were times when he became defiant and didn't want to do anything to help his younger brothers. He loved hauling his friends in the car.

One mistake that I think that my mother made was giving him so much access to the family car. She included him on the car insurance because he was under twenty-five years of age. I do confess that he kept the car looking nice and clean. It always looked new inside and out. He did this to impress his friends and people in the neighborhood. He felt as if he owned the car because my mother would allow him to drive to school while he was in high school. My mother finally realized that it was a mistake to allow him to drive the car so often because he was hauling his friends around and they smoked marijuana in the car. Randall also smoked cigarettes which was a bad habit to develop in high school. Marijuana does smell worse than cigarettes. I could always tell when Randall and his friends were high, the car reeked of the smell of marijuana and their eyes were red. Everything was funny to them and their appetite increased for sweet things. I don't know why my mother didn't do anything about his conduct in our car when she saw all the cigarette burns on the seat. My brother only cared about his personal use of the family car. He shouldn't have been allowed to smoke in the car let alone smoke marijuana in the car.

Randall wrecked two of the family cars that my mother allowed him to drive. My mother had Triple AAA insurance during this time (1970–1975). The insurance company informed my mother that Randall had to be removed from the insurance and that he couldn't drive any more vehicles that were insured by Triple AAA. He was very upset and it was getting close to his graduation. By that time, I had my driver's license and I didn't have to depend on him to take me anywhere else again. He hated that he couldn't drive the family car anymore. This made me happy because I could drive. When he graduated he decided to go into the Navy. We all were relieved when he went into the service because he couldn't even get insurance when he graduated from high school because of his bad driving record. I was so glad when he couldn't drive the family car anymore. I thought he made a smart decision by going into the Armed Forces after high school. My other siblings were ecstatic that he was leaving Gary for the service.

He stayed in the Navy for four years and he was stationed in Jacksonville, Florida. He continued to smoke marijuana in the service. He also had the same girlfriend that he had in high school. They married during his last year in the Navy. They moved back to Gary and during that time, he was drinking alcohol heavily along with smoking pot. He never stopped smoking pot. He was able to obtain a very good job after leaving the Navy. They gave priority to men who have served their country. With his alcohol abuse and drug abuse, he lost that job working for an electric company. His wife did everything that she could to prevent him from losing that job at a well-known electrical power company in Gary. My brother went on to have four children with his wife. Their marriage ended in divorce because of his continued use of alcohol and other drugs. He was very abusive to his wife. He managed to get another good job at a well-known company in Gary. That job didn't last because of his alcoholism and drug usage. For all the things that kept happening to him, he did seem resilient. He was to obtain another good-paying job after job.

When he lost all of his jobs and his wife, he never amounted to anything. He was a good manipulator and he used a lot of people during his life. He lied about everything and at one point, he was almost homeless. My father did allow him to live with him around 2005 and that didn't last. My father had to put him out of the house. My father caught him smoking crack cocaine in his basement with some shady characters that had criminal records. They all were involved in crime to maintain their drug habits. I warned my father about allowing another brother to live with him. There are things in life that you have to learn the hard way even if it means jeopardizing your well-being and safety. Hanging around drug addicts is very dangerous because they will kill you and do anything to get more drugs. My father didn't realize the severity of his drug use and crack cocaine use.

Randall had destroyed his body for years with alcohol, marijuana, and crack cocaine which eventually led to his demise. He passed away in 2018 from congestive heart failure. The doctor informed the family that he needed a heart transplant years ago. His heart was destroyed by substance abuse and it was worn out. I made an effort to help in 2014 when he was renting an apartment. I gave him furniture and provided paint for his apartment. I even purchased him a new refrigerator. He never appreciated any of the things that I did for him. I did ask for a small amount of compensation for some of the things that I had given him. I never received a dime from him and my father tried to help him also.

He was always under the impression that someone owed him something in life. My mother did spoil him. She could have held back on giving him some of the things that made him feel that he was God's gift to the world. He was a liar and he used so many people in his life and he could have done more for his children. He wasn't a good role model for his kids. They were lucky to have a mother that always had a job and she did more for those children than he did. There are some bad people in the world and there still are some good people still left in the world. I placed him on the bad person's list because of how he conducted himself throughout his life. He didn't have to treat people in a certain and negative way. He made some bad decisions and they ended up catching up with him as he got older. He seemed to maintain the same mindset about every situation.

My mother and father endured a lot of suffering and pain because of his actions and behavior growing up. My father despised him as an adult and I could see why. He always made everything about him and his friends. His friends growing up were more important to him than me and my other brothers that grew up in the same household. I don't hold any grudges against anyone. There were times when I contemplated in my mind was there anything that my parents could have done to make his outlook look more promising? I am sure that drugs and alcohol played a very important role in his destiny. What would have been his outcome if he never got involved in marijuana, crack cocaine, and other abusive drugs? I guess we will never know. It was a rumor that before he had the last heart-attack he was up all night smoking crack cocaine that might have contributed to his massive heart attack. They found him lying on the kitchen floor unconscious. He lasted a week in the hospital before he passed. At his funeral, I came across a lot of his former classmates and I couldn't recognize half of them. They looked older than my parents did because of the years of drug abuse. They used more drugs than any class that had graduated from my former high school. They looked like characters from the movie: *The Living Dead*!

<u>Comments:</u> I truly wished that I could have done something to make his life better when he got out of the Navy. He had developed behaviors that I have always questioned as an adult and a child. I still can't understand why my mother would allow him to do drugs in our household. You have to wonder why these things contributed to his demise. If he grew up in a different environment maybe the outcome would have been different. I regretted that he got my other brothers involved in drugs and some of my cousins.

Larry

Larry was the baby in our family. He was composed of a very outgoing personality and he had friends in high school. Sports was something that he enjoyed and he played basketball and football in high school. Larry did attend college and finish college and he did find a very good job. His degree in college was in Criminal Justice. He started smoking pot in high school also. I can recall him losing his job because he was caught with drugs but he eventually recovered from this incident and found another job. The last child in our house and he was spoiled rotten by my parents. As he got older, we drifted apart because of reasons mentioned in his narrative.

Larry was the youngest in a family of nine. He was my father's child and not my mother's husband's child. He was also a piece of work. I thought that I was very close to Larry growing up. In some respects, he looked up to me. Our age difference was about four years. I discovered that he started smoking pot in the tenth grade but it didn't seem to be an issue because he didn't seem to indulge as much as some of my other brothers. I can recall many times when he was in the basement smoking pot with some of his friends and my brother (Randall) who introduced my other brothers to marijuana.

Larry started on a very good note. He graduated from high school. He was always active in intramural sports as a child in elementary school. They always had football teams and he also played basketball in high school. His team won the state championship in 1980. This was a big accomplishment for him. Playing basketball kept him out of trouble and out of the streets in

Gary. When he played basketball for Gary High School, he didn't play in every game. The coach did allow him to play in most of the games. There was so much talent in Gary.

He attended Purdue University and obtained a BS in Criminal Justice. While he was attending college, I allowed him to live with me in South Bend and I didn't charge him rent because he was in college. He already had some serious expenses with tuition etc. He was able to work part-time at Burger King while attending college. For some reason, I felt an obligation to help him go to school and provide a place for him to live for four years. We had a good relationship for many years.

Once he graduated, he was lucky to land a job with the Juvenile Detention Center in South Bend. He wanted to work in a community that was close to where he grew up. He was doing well and making good money working for the City of South Bend. He wasn't married at that time and he didn't have any children. I can't remember if he had a girlfriend at the time. I can remember during that time; we were living in an apartment complex when he finished college. Then he decided to rent an apartment in the same complex. He moved out of my apartment. He decided to date a girl that he went to high school with. They moved in together. When I graduated from graduate school, I moved to South Bend in 1984 and accepted a nice-paying job.

I decided to rent a home in a different neighborhood and at that point, Larry didn't want to live with his girlfriend anymore. I allowed him to follow me and move in with me again. He lived with me in the home that I was renting. My older brother from

Gary wanted Dwayne, my brother in **Chapter One** to come and live with us. This was a mistake. Drug dealers had a hit out on Dwayne. They thought he would be safe living with me and Larry in South Bend. We had some issues with Dwayne living with us, he didn't want to buy food or help with the rent. This was the behavior he had living in Gary in my childhood home with my other brothers and sister.

Honestly, I had enough with Larry and Dwayne living with me. I thought that they should have an apartment. It had come to a point where I felt like I was taking care of them. I wasn't married and I didn't have any children. There was a period where I wanted to live by myself without the responsibility of taking care of two brothers. They were forced to move. They lasted in an apartment for about six months. It is very difficult to live with someone when no one wants to pay the rent or pay any bills. They both were writing bad checks knowing that they didn't have money in their checking accounts. Dwayne was up to his old tricks of smoking crack cocaine. These incidents happened around 1986. Larry might have been smoking crack cocaine with Dwayne during this time. These incidents happened around 1986. Larry might have been smoking crack cocaine also.

I remember when I lived in my house with Dwayne and Larry, I came home and they were smoking crack cocaine with people that Larry worked with at the Juvenile Detention Center in my kitchen. This was when I told them that they had to move out of my house and because of all the problems and stress that they created living with me. A nut came to my house and kicked in my front door looking for Dwayne. I didn't own the house that I rented and I was good friends with the landlords. Dwayne moved back to Gary and Larry stayed in South Bend.

When things didn't work out with Dwayne and Larry, Larry was looking for a place to live after they lost their apartment. Larry wanted to come and live with me again. I decided that it wouldn't be in my best interest to allow him to live with me again. He eventually moved back to Gary. During the time that Larry lived with me in South Bend, I cosigned two automobiles for him. At that time, he was doing well and working and he was very productive. Being naïve, I cosigned another automobile for him. This was the worst mistake of my life. I found out that he was using this automobile to transport crack cocaine from Maine. Larry ruined and destroyed the car. It was in terrible shape and he stopped paying the car note. This placed me in a very bad legal situation where I didn't want to be. Larry didn't want to pay the car note and I was obligated to pay the car note because I co-signed for Larry to buy the car. There were many attempts to take the car back but the dealership didn't want the car back. The car was a lemon when Larry purchased it. How could I be so stupid as to co-sign another car for Larry?

When Larry moved back to Gary from South Bend, he was still working for the Juvenile Detention Center. I had no idea that the people he worked with were using crack cocaine. They were supposed to be role models for these juveniles. I was very disappointed in Larry knowing that he was involved in smoking crack cocaine and eventually selling it at the same time while he was working for the Juvenile Detention Center.

In 1989, Larry and his friends decided to drive to South Bend from Gary in the middle of the night. The time was around 2:00 A.M. They drove through an area that was a high traffic area for cops. They would always be looking for speeders in Gary. Larry was aware of this because he would drive back and forth from Gary to South Bend. A cop pulled them over and found some ounces of crack cocaine. When the cops stopped them, they were trying to hide the drug but that didn't happen. Larry was with his friends, Nathaniel and Donald. No one would take responsibility for crack cocaine. Larry was charged and he had to get an attorney to represent him while his buddies walked away clean from this incident. It was apparent that the crack cocaine belonged to Larry in the first place. He was lying to everyone including the lawyer that the crack cocaine didn't belong to him.

During that time, Larry was the only one that had a decent job and he was doing well working for the Juvenile Detention Center. You can't have a criminal record working for the Department of Corrections. Larry wound up losing the good job that he had. We never found out who the drugs belonged to but Larry was charged with possession. I thought that it was Larry's crack cocaine.

As this entire ordeal unfolded with Larry, I was still responsible for the car that I cosigned for Larry. He was adamant about not paying any more car payments. I was stuck with the balance of the car payments even though the automobile was returned to the dealership in terrible condition. I was appalled that Larry didn't want to honor his agreement with me and continue to pay the car note. He was done with any obligation that tied him to that car. It was a mistake to do a favor for him.

Larry was able to get another job working for a baby food company. It wasn't the ideal job but it paid the bills. When he was on trial for drug possession, he convinced the lawyer that the drugs were not his drugs. The attorney fought and challenged the charge against my brother. My brother wasn't honest with his attorney during the entire process according to the others that were accused of the drugs not being theirs. At one point. I almost talked to the attorney and I wanted to tell him the truth. The attorney arrived at a plea deal and my brother was placed on probation for a couple of years. He couldn't afford a regular lawyer and he was appointed a lawyer by the courts. Those court-appointed attorneys don't seem to work very hard for clients. You get better representation for your bucks when you have to pay for an attorney out of your pocket.

The car that I cosigned was still a thorn in my back. Larry continued to work for the baby food company. I found out later that he sued the Juvenile Detention Center for firing him and won a $10,000 settlement but never informed me of the settlement while I continued to pay the car note for a couple of years. I informed him that if he doesn't pay this debt that I was going to get a lawyer. What made me so upset was when he got the settlement from the Juvenile Detention Center for losing his job, he didn't want to pay the delinquent money owed on the car that I cosigned for. He had no intention of telling me about the settlement as I continued to pay for the car. The way that I heard about the settlement was through my father. My father couldn't understand why he didn't pay the balance owed on the car. He sued the Juvenile Detention Center for unlawful firing and won. I could understand why the center would let him go because you can't be charged with a crime when you are working for the Department of Justice. It is unethical and insubordination to have a record working for the State.

Then I decided to take matters into my own hands because the dealership was suing me. After all, I cosigned for the car and they wanted their money even though the car was returned and unsellable. I was served a summons and I had to appear in court after I had already paid about $1000.00 of my own money against the debt. I had to sue my brother so that I wouldn't have to continue to pay for a car that was repossessed. My lawyer was able to get a judgment against my brother and his wages were garnished until the remainder of the car note was paid in full. I had done a favor for my brother twice and he still refused to take any responsibility for the car that he drove and destroyed. I was appalled by his behavior and believe me I never cosigned on a loan again for anyone.

Larry eventually married and had two children and moved to a town closer to his new job. To this very day, he is still working for the baby food company. He eventually divorced his wife and lives with one of his daughters. We don't have a good relationship with each other. It was destroyed years ago. I have tried for many years to make amends with him but for some reason, it never came to fruition.

Comments: The saddest thing about this situation is the way that people are treated when they bend over backward to help their siblings. The problem that I had with Larry is that he always felt that the world owed him something and that is why he took advantage of so many people including me. I wasn't my brother's keeper and I guess I was wrong for trying to do so. I was naïve to think that my brothers would try to take advantage of me.

Charlie

Charlie was very quiet in high school. He was respectful to others. I can't remember if he ever had a job but he always lived with his mother as an adult. He might have played sports in high school but he attended a different high school than I did. Charlie was the youngest in his family also. He grew up not having a positive role model in his life. The father was never at home and when he wasn't at home, he was chasing women. We played together as kids and drifted apart as we got older. His story is very interesting and you can read about him in the narrative below.

Charlie was a cousin of mine. We grew up primarily in the same neighborhood. He is the son of one of my mother's sisters. They all moved to Indiana from the South looking for husbands and a better way of life. Charlie was the same age as my brother Larry. We were very close to our aunts and our cousins. I have some fond memories of all of us growing up together in the town of Gary. When you have a lot of cousins around growing up, it gives you something to look forward too and you always had fun growing up with your cousins.

Charlie graduated from Mona Shores High School in 1981. He was an average student but he didn't have any ambitions to pursue college. He lived with my aunt Glenda and his father. He has another brother and two sisters that passed in recent years. They all graduated from high school as well. None of them went to college except for one sister. They were glad to graduate from high school.

I will give you some information about his family's background. My aunt Glenda was a nurse's assistant and she worked in a local hospital during the early '70s until retirement in the late nineties. Her husband had different jobs but never maintained a consistent job that I can remember. He was one of the uncles that I mentioned in **Chapter One** that had a girlfriend while he was still married to my aunt. I am sure that my aunt was aware of his infidelity. How could she not know? We all knew everyone in our community. The problem that I had with her husband was that he treated his girlfriend's children better than my cousins. We would attend sporting events in Gary and he would show up with his girlfriend's kids. He eventually passed in the seventies from an automobile accident coming home. He had substance abuse issues. He drank alcohol heavily for most of his life.

Charlie didn't have a good role model to follow or someone that he could look up to. My uncle was always gone and he spent more time with his girlfriend that is still alive today. None of his brothers set a positive example for him to follow. He did have a stepbrother that attended college. He was an alcoholic. I can remember him babysitting for my aunt many times.

I can recall Charlie and his brother getting involved with drugs in high school also. They smoked marijuana with my brother Randall, Dwayne, and Larry. For all that I knew, my brother Randall probably got them started on marijuana also. Pot smoking was something that seemed so normal because everyone was smoking pot but me. I never had any desire to smoke marijuana as much as I was around it. Charlie's pot habit eventually led to stronger drugs such as crack cocaine. This was the next step in trying other drugs. I am sure that he did crack cocaine with his brother Kyle. Their sister also did crack cocaine. Her name was Katrina. She and Kyle were twins. I will discuss Katrina later.

My aunt Glenda never seemed to push these kids to do anything. She allowed all of them to live with her up to adulthood. They would have small jobs every once in a while. None of them seemed to hold a steady job. They had one sister by the name of Wilma and I think that she might have gone to college for one year. I thought that my aunt should have pushed them a little harder to pursue their dreams. They didn't get any motivation from their father.

It was obvious that Charlie was the baby of the family and spoiled rotten. My aunt allowed him to do whatever he wanted to do. I wish I could remember if he ever held any kind of job after he graduated from high school. I have never known him to hold down a job. When I would visit my aunt and cousins, he was always just hanging around. There wasn't anything exciting about him. My aunt gave him everything that he wanted. This might have contributed to his demise and lack of ambition in life. Charlie's demeanor was very low key. Nothing seemed to excite him but smoking crack cocaine.

His use of crack cocaine made him lazy and not motivated to do anything but hang around with thugs who helped him support his drug habit. He might have been on some kind of disability but I didn't know what for if that was the case. If you have someone providing a roof over your head and supplying you with food, why would you want to work? Charlie was born around 1962. In the early 2000s, he was still living with my aunt without a job. My aunt eventually retired and she allowed him to still live at home. His brother Kyle was also living with my aunt.

One time Kyle and Charlie got into a serious fight and Kyle hit him in the head with a blunt object. He didn't hit him hard enough to kill him. This assault was kind of serious and for some reason or another, Kyle wasn't charged for the assault. They both were using crack cocaine at that time. My aunt might have known that they smoked marijuana but I don't think that she knew that they were using crack cocaine. She should have put both of them out of her house. Wilma had moved out of the house a long time ago and got married to a very nice young man. She died in 2019 from congestive heart failure. Her sister Katrina lived in the house with my aunt until she passed in 2008.

For some strange reason, I knew that Charlie was going to be a problem for my aunt one day because of his record of bad conduct. He had a lot of issues with the cops and my aunt was always bailing him out. Charlie never learned from his transgressions. I did wish that he would have gone to college and it would have been great if he could have held down one good job. He wasn't a bad human being and I remember that he was nice to all of his cousins growing in Gary. When you do drugs, it does change your personality and how you react to others. Some people are violent and treat people awful. Charlie had developed a serious drug problem while living with my aunt.

He got himself into some serious trouble and there was no way that anyone could save him and get him out of some predicaments that he got himself into. I had heard that his relationship with my aunt had become volatile. We heard that he had hit her a couple of times and he demonstrated some violent behavior towards her. This is why his brother hit him in the head with a deadly object. When you have two crack heads living in the same household, you are going to have some serious problems. Some drugs do alter your personality. This is what happened to Charlie.

A neighbor was walking through the neighborhood of my aunt, where Charlie lived. She would always stop and speak to my aunt through her porch as she did her morning walks in the neighborhood. She looked on the porch when she arrived at my aunt's house. Then she saw my aunt lying on the porch in a puddle of blood unconscious. She called 911 and my aunt was rushed to the hospital. Aftėr she arrived at the hospital, she was in critical condition for a couple of weeks. When I had spoken with my sister, she was allowed to visit my aunt at the hospital. My sister informed me that my aunt's face was smashed like a pancake and you couldn't recognize who she was.

After the incident, Charlie and Kyle were nowhere to be found. I think that Kyle was living with his girlfriend at the time. Charlie and my aunt were the only ones living in my aunt's house. People started to suspect Charlie right away. They were looking for Charlie for a couple of days to ask him if he knew about the incident with my aunt. There was a police investigation and the truth was revealed. Charlie was the cause of my aunt's incident. Charlie had come home very high on drugs and demanded some money from my aunt. She refused to give him any money. I think she was at the end of her ropc and refused. She refused to give him one penny. It was confirmed that Charlie went into the kitchen and grabbed a cast iron skillet from one of the cabinets in the kitchen and struck my aunt a couple of times in the head until she was unconscious. He left her in the house in fear because of what he had done to my aunt. He was a man on the run high as a kite running scared. I know that Charlie was scared and I had never known him to be that violent towards my aunt after living with her for many years. He had never known any other home than where he grew up.

When this incident occurred, Charlie probably was strung out and high on crack cocaine and he might have snapped when my aunt Glenda didn't give him the money. His mind was all messed up. I could never imagine him doing this to his mother or my aunt, sober, or high on drugs. This was one of the saddest and disturbing disasters that have ever happened to any relative or anyone in my family. My aunt stayed in the hospital for a couple of months but she eventually died from the trauma to the head. This was a tragic experience.

Charlie was convicted of murder. He has been in prison for the last twelve years with no hope of parole. We never thought that something like this would ever happen to our aunt and we never thought that one of our cousins would be the blame for such a terrible crime to a relative. This entire story was a tragic end for Charlie and the siblings that were left after my aunt passed. There is only one child left in this family. He still lives in the same house where my aunt lived. That home has some terrible memories. My cousin is on his last leg. There is no way that I could continue to live in that house after losing my mother and all of my other siblings. I did see him at my brother's funeral in 2018 and he didn't look that great.

Comments: So, this is the way you pay a parent back after that parent has done everything in the world to make sure that you have food and a decent place to stay. In a million years, I never thought that I would be the author of any of these stories that I am sharing with you. Cocaine still is a destructive drug; it destroys families and human beings. During this entire incident, I lost a beautiful aunt and a cousin that will never get out of prison. I fear anyone in prison at this time in history because of the spreading and impact that the Coronavirus has had in the United States.

Katrina

Katrina was just a very nice and pleasant young lady. We did so many things together in high school and she was a good dancing partner at dances in high school. She loved to sing and she could sing but nothing that would turn her into a star. People just adored her because of her warm personality. Katrina held a job as an adult for a short period. One incident that I will never forget about her is when a high school girl thought she was messing around with her boyfriend. This was during the time of prom and her senior year in high school. This girl came to her home to threaten her to leave her boyfriend alone and she started a fight with Katrina and scarred her face pretty bad with a knife which made it impossible for her to attend the prom her senior year. Some of the scars didn't disappear and she had some beautiful skin. This was a devastating experience for her and my aunt was upset that something like this would happen to her. It was hard to believe that this girl had the nerve to come and start a fight with my cousin at her own home. This girl and her family were known for fighting and causing chaos in the neighborhood. Her family had a reputation for violence. You can learn more about her in the narrative below.

Katrina was one of my cousins that I grew up with in Gary. Her mother and my mother were sisters. They all came to Indiana from Mississippi. As I had said earlier, they all were looking for husbands and they wanted to get out of the South. It was kind of sweet having an aunt live across the street. This was very convenient for all the cousins to play with each other. Katrina was the sister of Charlie and Kyle in the narrative under Charlie.

Katrina was the same age as Randall so they would hang around each other growing up in high school. It never dawned on me the reason that Katrina would hang around Randall. They all would be smoking pot together. In high school, we would go to dances together and we always had dancing partners throughout high school. She would be in our basement smoking pot with Randall and some of my other cousins that indulged in marijuana smoking in high school. People seem to do the same thing in high school. I never got interested in marijuana. Keeping a straight head was important to me growing up and when I entered high school.

She graduated from high school and she eventually went on to obtain a job after high school. I think that she might have taken a few college classes at our local Community College. So many high school students went to Community College after high school. They wanted to see if they could be successful and eventually go on to a bigger university. We all had some college dreams. To obtain these dreams was a challenge for most people especially African Americans. College was readily available but so many African Americans found employment in factories in the late seventies. Katrina didn't seem that interested in going to college.

Some students decided to continue to live at home with their parents and were content with working in factories or other businesses that would hire them. Katrina worked for a company that made candy. The company was very popular in the area and her sister even worked for the company. The job that she had paid enough where she could have her apartment like her other sister but she decided to stay at home and live with my aunt. She slept in the same bedroom that she shared with her sister Wilma in high school.

I can remember when she purchased her first vehicle and she loved driving around in the neighborhood showing it to everyone. Her first car was a Corvette. It wasn't completely new but when she purchased the car, it was in excellent condition. No one could afford a new Corvette because they were very expensive.

She continued to work for this candy company and continued smoking pot which eventually led to a habit of smoking crack cocaine like her brother Charlie and Kyle. I am sure that they all used this drug in my aunt's house. Katrina would come around my brothers and they would still smoke marijuana together but I have never seen them smoke crack cocaine but everybody knew they all were users.

As Katrina continued to live with her mom and two other brothers, she eventually lost her job at the candy factory because another company was buying the company that she worked for about eight years. At that point, she never found another job and continued to live off her mother as her brothers did. When you have someone taking care of you, there is no ambition to find another job.

Something tragically happened to Katrina while she was on a bus trip to Detroit with some friends. I can't remember what sparked her to go on a bus trip with a couple of friends. People knew that this trip involved heavy partying, drinking, and doing drugs that were illegal at the time. The period was around 2001. As the bus was driving to Detroit, they looked at the back of the bus to find that Katrina had slumped over and was unconscious. Passengers on the bus didn't know what was going on and they couldn't revive her. They managed to get her to a local hospital and found out that she had a stroke. She stayed in the hospital for months without any positive signs of recovery and she went into a coma. She was transferred to a nursing home with the hope that she might eventually come out of the coma in Gary. I went to see her and she was still in a comatose state for about six years never responding to treatment or never waking up again.

My aunt was hopeful and determined that she would eventually recover from the serious stroke that placed her in a coma for many years. We all were supporting my aunt with prayer and hoping that Katrina would beat this serious medical condition. They found out what had caused the stroke. A friend on the bus informed us that she was smoking crack cocaine during the entire trip to Detroit. Her heart was seriously damaged by drug usage for many years. I always thought that she only smoked marijuana but I was dead wrong.

This entire tragedy was a shock to my aunt and all of our relatives. We never could imagine something like this happening to one of our cousins. Katrina was a very nice person and everybody liked her. She never got married or had any children. She had a couple of boyfriends throughout high school and while she was working for the candy company. I truly wished that she would have had a better life. She got caught up in using drugs in the same manner that my brothers did and others that lived in Gary, Indiana.

She passed in a nursing home around 2003. We all attended her funeral and I was a pallbearer at the event. The funeral was very sad and my aunt took her death hard along with her only sister. Drugs have destroyed so many families during the '70s and into the '90s. Reflecting on this story always brings tears to my eyes because as a cousin, I wanted something better for my cousin and all of my siblings. Some of the choices that they made led to death or being locked up in prison.

<u>Comments:</u> We all are entitled to make our own choices in life. You can have good parents and still make bad decisions. When you hang around the wrong people, you tend to pick up the bad habits that they have. My brother wasn't a good influence and I still think he might have had something to do with my cousin doing drugs. He didn't discourage her not to do drugs especially when he was doing them himself.

William

William would hang around with my brother Larry. He had an inferiority complex about being short and he had a short fuse. It didn't take that much to get him to explode in a mean and nasty manner. His father was scared of him and that is why he sent him from Texas to live with his grandfather. He started using drugs in high school also. He was academically challenged and he almost didn't graduate from high school. One thing that I did like about him was his laugh which was kind of intriguing. The laugh was unique and you would never think that he had a temper. It is sad what happened to him.

William was a cousin of my father's siblings. He was the same age as my younger brother (Larry). They graduated from the same high school in 1981. Larry hung around with William during high school. I always had a problem with William because he had one of the worst tempers that I had ever experienced. It didn't take that much to set him off. He was short and for some strange reason, this seemed to bother him and affected his personality.

He was sent to Indiana around 1973. After all, his father was scared of him as a child because he had some serious emotional issues that were frightening. William had another brother that was about his age. They both grew up in Tyler, Texas. Their father just couldn't handle two boys. William was sent to Indiana to live with his grandparents. This was very challenging for the grandparents. They did the best that they could by allowing him to live with them until he finished high school. He got started using drugs in ninth grade which was just marijuana. He eventually started using other drugs in high school.

William would hang out with my brother Larry and they did so many things in high school. I thought that William admired my brother for some unexplainable reason. William spent time at our home in Gary. My mother seemed to like him as well. What we didn't know that he had was a dark side and eventually, we realized that his dark side was the temper that he had through high school. This is one of the reasons why his father sent him to live with his grandparents from Tyler, Texas.

When William graduated from high school, his grandfather told him that he needed to move back to Tyler, Texas. We don't know the circumstances as to why he had to move back to Tyler. I am sure that it had something to do with his conduct while he was living with his grandparents. They knew that he was involved in drugs and we had heard that he was selling drugs before he moved back to Tyler Texas. He wasn't interested in going to college. Any College would be challenging because he barely made it through high school. He didn't pass that many classes but he did graduate on time. My brother Larry was much smarter than William through high school. I am sure my brother was upset when he moved back to Tyler. They both graduated in 1981.

His father didn't want him to come back to Texas because he didn't get along with his brother Reggie. The father could hardly take care of himself let alone having two teenagers in the house. You can recall that the father was scared of William. The brother might have had issues with William also. William had been back in Texas for a year and a tragic accident happened at their home in Texas. When William moved back to Texas, he was strung out on crack cocaine and he used it heavily when he moved back to Texas. His father was aware of his drug habit but allowed him to do anything that he wanted. He knew that William came back to Texas that he couldn't control him or advise him.

The drug usage caused him to change his personality and he was just a mean person and he didn't get along with Reggie and his father. They lived in fear with him in the house in Texas. William got into an altercation with Reggie and William strangled his brother to death. His drug usage and temper had something to do with him killing his brother. This incident occurred in 1983 and William was convicted of first-degree murder and was sentenced to life in prison. His father eventually passed around 1990. William had a few cousins that lived in Houston, Dallas, and Tyler, Texas. He has been in prison for over thirty years without the chance of parole. This was a tragedy for everyone and no one ever thought that William would kill his flesh and blood. His brother's death had something to do with drugs. He killed his brother over drugs which continues to be a problem for some blacks that are involved in selling and using illegal drugs other than marijuana. One of the best things that helped some blacks was when marijuana became legal in some states. The incarcerations started to decrease with the legalization of marijuana.

Comments: We knew that William had a bad temper but we never thought that he would kill his only brother. When he was convicted, he showed no remorse at his trial. He just accepted what he had done and went straight to prison. It was sad what he had done and it left a mark on the family and all of his relatives.

Rosie and Richard

Rosie came from a family of very smart people. Her mother was a teacher's aide and her father always held down a job. She was very popular in high school and she became a cheerleader. Her personality was always upbeat and she had a contagious laugh. In high school, she looked a lot older than her age was. I had never known her to cheat people and run scams until she met her boyfriend, Richard. She got involved with him right out of high school. He was a drug dealer and he got Rosie into prostitution and other illegal things. He was the worst thing that could have happened to her. The interest in boys came at a very early age in high school. Rosie had a sister that she was very close too along with two brothers that loved her dearly. The boyfriend was a loser and I didn't know that much about him. They both were good dressers and had a taste for fashion. Rosie would have been very successful in college and she could have made something out of herself. Once you get hooked up with the wrong crowd, this contributes to your downfall in this life. It is very hard to break bad habits.

I am glad that she didn't get pregnant like some of the other girls in the neighborhood.

This story is about a couple that worked together as a team scamming people and using people to get ahead by selling drugs and the involvement of prostitution. First, let's talk about Rosie. Rosie lived in East Park Manor as I stated in **Chapter One**. She had another sister and two brothers. Her parents were decent people. The mother worked in the public school system as a paraprofessional. Her father worked in a foundry. When they lived in The Projects, this was a pleasant place to live.

I thought that Rosie was a nice person and she was the same age as my brother Larry. They both attended elementary through high school together. Rosie was always over at our house and she would also spend time in our basement smoking marijuana along with my brother Larry. This is what most high school students did. Larry might have dated Rosie in high school. Rosie's main objective was to finish high school like some of the other residents that lived in East Park Manor. She was a cheerleader in high school. Girls enjoyed being cheerleaders because they felt they stood above some of the other girls in their class.

Rosie graduated from high school in 1981. She was pretty smart and I think that she was in the top ten of her class when she graduated. We never heard her discuss any plans of going to college. She would have been very successful because of her success in high school. I think that she landed a job after high school. She continued to indulge herself in drugs and I think that her marijuana led her to use other drugs. Rosie always dated older guys in high school. I can recall her going with one of my older brother's classmates. That didn't last that long because she wanted to date older men and more sophisticated men. This might have contributed to her downfall in life. She also looked older.

There was a rumor going around that when she finished high school that she was tricking and doing some prostitution. This was verified by someone very close to her. She started dating this creep that was known as a dope pusher and he sold many different kinds of illegal drugs. People knew what people did in these towns where the heavy use of drugs was prevalent. We think that it was her boyfriend Richard that got her into prostitution. People would see Richard and her around town, they always had on the most expensive-looking clothes. Richard always wore a suit as if he was a pastor of a church. He was fifteen years older than Rosie. This didn't seem to bother Rosie because of her love for older men. It was known that she would set people up to be robbed. She and her boyfriend worked together scamming people. I guess she made good money selling drugs and prostitution. Richard had Rosie do things that were totally against her character. She was a grown-up during this time and there wasn't anything that her sister or her parents could do to persuade her to change her lifestyle. Rosie was very close to the only sister that she had. They were inseparable in high school and growing up in The Projects.

I graduated from graduate school in 1981 and moved to Florida right out of graduate school. I kept in contact with people in Gary and some of my brothers. My cousin moved down to Florida with me. We would always want to know what was going on in Gary and I could talk to some of my family and my dad who still lived in my hometown. When I lived in Florida, I was living in a Boarding House until I found a permanent home. We did have access to a telephone. It was nice to have my cousin with me in Florida because I had never been to Florida before. Two minds work better than one and I needed someone to help me drive when I moved to Florida. I also need someone to help me pay the rent in Florida because it was pretty expensive. Things didn't work out for me and my cousin and that is a story for another book.

We just happened to call home on a particular night. We were missing our relatives and I wanted to talk to one of my brothers. They were living in my childhood home with some of my other brothers. My brother Larry said over the phone that he had some sad news to tell me. He informed me that Rosie and her boyfriend Richard were killed by some drug dealers. Larry said that they were walking on a tightrope because they would cheat people out of money and they orchestrated some very bad drug deals. Someone had put out a hit on them for their terrible deeds to others. They were kind of assassinated and there was a rumor circulating in Gary that Rosie begged and pleaded for her life. I would never want to place myself in that kind of situation. Larry was very hurt because he grew up with Rosie and they had dated in high school. This has been the demise of so many drug dealers and anyone involved in crime. It eventually catches up to them and the outcome is dreadful.

The funeral was sad for both Rosie and Richard and it was a double funeral. They both were dressed in very expensive clothing that they wore when they were still alive. When they were living, they were very good dressers. It was obvious that they knew fashion and they looked like they had money even if it was from the selling of drugs and other illegal things. This was a tragedy for Rosie's family and our family because we were so close. What a way to die in this world and we wouldn't want to wish this kind of death on anyone. Our former classmate was murdered and the community was upset about this tragedy.

Comments: This is one story that I hated telling because of the people involved. We knew of Rosie's boyfriend. Rosie meant so much to us because we grew up together. When we travel down the wrong road, things of this nature occur. I thought that Rosie would fare so much better in life because she was very smart in high school. Her sister is still alive and her two brothers didn't get involved in drugs. Her sister was average in school and she did smoke pot and she might have smoked crack cocaine.

The Postman and His Wife (The Postman Always Rings Twice)
These two people, I didn't get to know that well. The postman's name is Gregory and his wife's name is Sandra. Greg delivered my mail in Gary, Indiana. I thought that he was a respectful human being because he always talked to me during his deliveries. We never did anything together but I am sure that it would have been fun going out to lunch with him and his wife. He had a nice persona that was inviting and kind. I guess you can't judge a book by its cover.

This story evolved around 1992 and the people that I am going to discuss, I wasn't close to. There was no connection with them as with others listed in my narratives. The Postman was the man who delivered my mail every day while living in South Bend, Indiana. During this time, I was working as a professional at one of the libraries in the area. This was my second professional job after moving back from Florida. When I lived in Florida, I had developed a very contentious relationship with my cousin that I had move to Florida with me in 1981. I decided to leave Florida even though I enjoyed working for the Palm Beach County Library System.

In South Bend, there was a rumor going around and an investigation was going on at the Post Office. People were saying that the post office had an employee that was delivering drugs to customers on his routes every day. The Post Office couldn't catch or pin down anyone for delivering cocaine to their customers. This was an African American male but during the time of the investigation, they didn't know what ethnic group the suspect belonged to. I suspect that they did have a clue that it might be someone of color. This wasn't a stereotype about Blacks. Many Blacks worked for the Post Office during this period.

The postman's name was Gregory and I thought he was a nice gentleman because he would always speak to me if I would run into him delivering the mail. Cordial to his customers and he would always speak to his customers. The people in our neighborhood had nothing but good things to say about him because he always delivered the mail on time. There weren't any complaints about his delivery of the mail. He was my mailman for about four years. Who would have ever suspected that he would be involved in something illegal? I guess he was running a racket in South Bend selling cocaine and other illegal drugs. Marijuana was illegal at the time along with other drugs.

It was stated the FBI had been following him for about a year but could never catch him doing anything illegal in the community. He had been delivering large amounts of crack cocaine to his postal customers. The FBI decided to place a decoy where he was delivering mail. They placed someone at the residence of one of his customers. This guy was supposed to buy some drugs from Gregory along with providing drugs to his regular customer at the residence. The FBI forced themselves into the residence and caught him as he was delivering drugs to his customers. They found him with three large bags of crack cocaine. Gregory said that it was a set-up and he was framed. Gregory's mailbag was loaded with cocaine and other drugs.

Gregory was arrested and the Post Office discovered that his wife was stealing Social Security checks. She sorted mail at the Post Office. Her name was Sandra. The FBI found out that she had stolen over 200 Social Security Checks and she found some way to cash every one of those checks. Gregory was selling drugs on his mailman's route and his wife worked inside of the Post Office stealing Social Security checks. It was hard to believe this conduct unfolded right in front of our eyes. I thought Gregory was a God-fearing Christian. I was deceived about my feelings about him. He and his wife Sandra were convicted and they served a twenty-year term in prison. This became a Headline in Gary. They might be out of prison now.

People are very clever when it comes to committing unlawful crimes and selling illegal drugs. They both had great careers in the Postal Services. It was obvious that they were driven by greed and making as much money as possible. You lose so much when you are caught doing unlawful things. Why take the risk? Two great careers were destroyed because of their ambition to sell drugs and steal Social Security Checks. It was indicated that they had children. What a sad story! There was some speculation that other mail carriers were involved in the same scheme but they never got caught. My theory has always been, no one knows you are a criminal until you have been caught.

Comments: You can be living on top of the world with a great income and have most of the things that you have always wanted in life. There is nothing wrong with obtaining things in life. If you are ambitious, you can obtain things without placing your integrity on the line by selling drugs and stealing things from hardworking Americans. To learn about this situation was very disturbing to me as a human being. Why do we jeopardize everything to do illegal things? These are questions that I am still trying to answer as an African American male.

Chapter Five

The Black Family

The dynamics of the Black Family have been kind of interesting. My family was kind of unusual as I had indicated in another chapter. When you have your mother going with a married man for years and almost being killed by her husband, you have to ask yourself what happened in that family. I thought that families were more intact with a mother and a father. Children hope that their parents would be married because this seems to make the family complete. This would entail having your father around all the time and he would be available to do more things with his sons etc. The girls would have the mother around so that they could do things that girls would do. The situation that my family was placed in was kind of strange. We were entitled to a normal family but that wasn't the case.

The thing that I found strange about my family was that my mother had been married and had four kids with her husband. You would have thought that they had the perfect family in the same manner that my cousins had a complete family with both parents working. My mother did have part-time and full-time jobs before she divorced her husband. Once my mother started having an affair with my father, this caused some chaos in the household.

Many things can cause infidelity in marriages. When my mother decided to divorce her husband, this did cause some problems for her children that she had with her husband. Children can pick up on problems in some marriages. I think that my older brothers and sisters were in elementary school when our mother had an affair with a married man. There are questions that I wish that I could have asked my mother as to why she started going with my father when she was happily married, or was she happily married? This was a discussion that we never had. It would have been nice to hear how she felt about that situation.

The problem that I had with my mother while she was going with a married man, I couldn't understand the situation. Once she got divorced and continued her relationship with my father (the married man), she was forced to go on welfare to take care of the children because basically, she became a single parent. My father was never forced to pay any kind of child support. This is one of the reasons why so many black families end up on welfare because fathers wouldn't pay child support. You have no other options if the mother isn't working. Some deadbeat dads have strayed away from their responsibilities as a parent. As a child, I wanted my mother to be married again. My mother just accepted the situation with my dad knowing that he wasn't going to leave his wife. It isn't for me to judge anyone but I wouldn't want to have children without a wife. I don't have children but I would have loved having a family. Every child is entitled to have two parents. Some circumstances can prevent this because of divorce. Things like this just happen and I don't think all these situations are deliberate. Once you are divorced, why go off and have five kids with a married man? This is something that I never got an answer from my mother. When women start having kids out of wedlock, this increases the percentages of single-parent homes and the percentage was 77 percent for black families around 2005 and has decreased somewhat over the years. This percentage was high compared to other ethnic groups during this period according to data.

As a black man, I always wanted to have children when married and the thought of having children without a wife was something that I couldn't bring myself to do. When I was in high school, I heard girls saying that in twelfth grade they were going to get pregnant on their prom night with their boyfriends. I found these comments to be ridiculous but these girls were serious and some of them did have babies in high school. In the black communities, this has been occurring since the early seventies to the early 2000s. When I was teaching in South Bend, Indiana, some of the students were pregnant but not that many as there were in the early '70s. Girls made comments about getting a hotel after the prom. Marriage has always been important to me and people should get married first before they ever think about having children. This is just my opinion. I was upset when some of the high school cheerleaders had babies. We thought that cheerleaders were supposed to be role models for the other students. Like I have stated many times in this book, I am trying to figure out and rationalize some of the behaviors of people that I grew up with as an African American man. If I was a parent during prom night, my daughter or son would have had to report home immediately after the prom was over. There wouldn't have been any exceptions. Parents have to establish the rules in the house, not their children.

Growing up in Gary and while in high school, I saw some of the challenges that these young girls were faced with. Some of them were still teenagers and they didn't have a clue as to how to raise a child. What happened was that the mother and other siblings ended up assisting them with raising a child while they were still in high school. A child alters a person's entire situation for the rest of their lives. Most of the responsibility or if not all the responsibility seems to always fall on the girl that had the child and not so much the father. This is why people should wait until they are grown and married to have children. If a girl is raped or in other circumstances, then you have to proceed accordingly. Girls that had babies in high school realized that raising a child was very challenging and some of them wished that they would have waited until they got married and finished college. This was something that I dreamed of when I was in high school. My priorities were going to college and establishing myself professionally before getting married and thinking about having children. Welfare was never going to be an option for me or SSI.

Black men do need to take more responsibility when they have children out of wedlock which I am totally against. When I was teaching in South Bend in the early eighties, a teacher told me that his son had eighteen children with five different women. After he made those comments to me, I couldn't believe that this man was telling me something like this. I would be embarrassed to share this information with anyone. This kind of behavior isn't acceptable and I told this man that he should have been doing more parenting and serving as a role model for his son. Oprah Winfrey did a show on men who had twenty and thirty children with women. This is not an exaggeration. These men were making comments and explaining why they couldn't pay any child support. This show might have been orchestrated for ratings. The men seemed to be telling the truth about their situations. You would have to say to yourself why do women fall into traps with these men and have children with them. As a woman, I would be very cautious going out with a man with a couple of kids unless I knew the circumstances of his situation. Some families are separated by divorce and this could be beyond the man or woman's control. I have known some women to trap a man by getting pregnant thinking that the man will marry them. They are delusional to have these kinds of thoughts and it might work in some situations.

In the early 2000s, I was very upset with my brother and sister-in-law when they allowed their daughter to have children while she was still living in their household. My niece was a high school student at the time. My brother and his wife had kids when they were married. They went together during their high school career. Some girls wanted to grow up too fast and some girls wanted children to validate their existence. When my niece started having children, I was living in South Bend but she was still living in Gary, Indiana. I honestly thought that my niece would go to college. This was my dream for her since some of my other nieces and nephews had attended college and graduated with successful careers. My niece always had a nasty attitude and you couldn't give her any advice. She had three children with her boyfriend that ended up going to jail and not being able to pay child support. Another situation that bothered me was that my ex-sister-in-law allowed her to stay in her home and develop a relationship with a married man. She had two children with a married man and he wasn't paying any child support. My niece was forced to go on some type of welfare because ADC didn't exist anymore. I thought her entire situation was kind of sad and she is still raising six children without a husband. A man doesn't want to marry a woman with six children and when most of them are from different men. All of my other nieces and nephews waited to have children when they were married.

Birth control wasn't as readily available as it is today during the '50s, '60s, and '70s. Others did take precautions in the early '50s, '60s, '70s, etc. by not having children without being married. Today, they have advanced methods in birth control and they even have things available for men to use to prevent them from impregnating women. The pressure has always been on women to take some kind of birth control. In the 2000s, people are having children because they want to have children. Some women have reverted to giving children up for adoption because they can't give a child the kind of lifestyle that they deserve. There is nothing wrong with adoption and others might give a child up for adoption because of rape etc. Some men stray away from using condoms at the expense of getting a woman pregnant. People have also said that birth control doesn't work and this is how they got pregnant. There are professional women having children without being married but they don't have to depend on welfare or section 8 housing that some women have to rely on for support when they aren't receiving any kind of child support from men whom they aren't married to.

The family has always been a crucial component of our heritage. It is the backbone of our existence past and present. Survival of our existence has always depended on the dynamics of the Black Family. Once there is a crack in the foundation, problems start to sneak up and disrupt the bedrock of our well-being. When slavery was introduced into the Americas, slaves would cling together for strength and survival. It was devastating when family members were separated and sold to different slave owners. This was detrimental to so many families during this period in American History. Slaves were thrown into slave auctions never seeing their immediate family ever again.

Once slavery was outlawed with the Emancipation Proclamation of 1862, slaves made many attempts to find their brothers and sisters so that they could reunite with them. Some former slaves were very successful and some weren't so successful. We had our issues growing up in Gary, Indiana but we kept our family structure intact. There were many times when I didn't want to be in the family because of the situation that was created by the conduct of my mother and father which I had alluded to earlier in this book. My parents provided us with what we needed even if we were on Aid for Dependent Children or welfare. There were times when we came up short but this didn't change our attitude or family dynamics. Love was a key component in the household which was created by my parents. They always placed us first and that would always entail making sure that we had enough to eat every day. Our situation could have been worse but they cared enough to provide for the family. My complaints were minor. My parents' moral compass came into question all the time because of the arrangement that they had. We were living in a single-parent home because my father lived with his wife and he would see us during the week and on the weekends. I know that it would have been difficult for my mother to raise nine children without any support from my father. Child support probably would have made a difference so that we wouldn't have to depend on welfare and later my brother's VA check that he received once a month. My mother depended on support from my brother who was in the U.S. Army.

Some people are born into poverty because of the conduct of their parents. Income inequality destroys some families. Multi-Generational Poverty has been an issue for Blacks for decades. This has caused a collapse in the structure of the family. As we examine the history of single-parent homes, in 2005 70 percent of black children were born to single mothers. This data was pulled from the Annie E. Casey Foundation. As you examine the statistics on (single) children in single-parent families by race (2009-2018) 65 percent of Blacks were living in single-parent homes compared to 15 percent of Asians with single-parent homes. See statistics below from (2009 – 2018). Some of the statistics haven't changed that much.

Children in single-parent families by race in the United States

American Indian	53% - 53%	2018
Asian and Pacific Islander	16% - 15%	2018
Black or African American	**67% - 65%**	**2018**
Hispanic or Latino	40% - 41%	2018
Non-Hispanic White	24% - 24%	2018

Blacks still account for the highest rates in single-parent households compared to other ethnic groups. This has been a serious issue and concern for blacks for many decades. This has opened the door to many problems for black families. Single mothers are more likely to be poor than married mothers. It bothered me that my mother didn't want to marry again in the same manner as her sisters and brothers. Our family was kind of short-changed after my mother divorced her husband and remained single with nine children. Poverty is a contagious disease and, in some cases, it is passed on to children of single mothers. The opportunities are limited in some single-parent homes. The future can be bleak for families with single-parent homes unless the parent has a decent job and a good income. Please don't get me wrong, there are a lot of successful households with single-parent homes. People are making better choices by going to college and seeking great job opportunities. I have a couple of friends that have been successful in raising one child without a husband.

All children should have the luxury of having both parents in the household. My brother divorced his first wife and they had two children and the children went on to college and were successful and married and had children. Your resources are more plentiful with two parents and your parents can acquire more things for the family. There are many things that two parents can provide for the family that are more bountiful for the children. Increased finances in the household give families the opportunities to save money and send their children to college. Home ownership doesn't seem to be an issue when your parents are married. You can provide more things for the family and you serve as role models for your children by holding down two full-time jobs.

We are a two-family nation. We are seeing that higher-income women wait to have children until they are married. Two parent-families seem to be thriving and are intact while some single-parent families struggle more and are broken. For some reason, African Americans fall more into the category of single-parent families according to the literature and data included in this narrative.

In the 1980s in the inner-city, the black family continued to crack. Child poverty was 20 percent and ran up to 22.7 percent in 1993. This made welfare dependency rise going from 2 million families in 1970 to 5 million by 1995, 65 percent of black children were being born to unmarried women. In Central Harlem, it was close to 80 percent around 1995. When these kinds of numbers are recorded, children were destined to grow up in poor households. They pass down the legacy of being a single parent to their children.

In the 2000s and before, society has come to the reality that some single mother families don't work. As I have stated before, some families have been successful with the help of grandparents and other family members. I have experienced some households where grandparents have gotten custody of children because of neglect and other reasons. This has never been the norm but families are chained to situations and habits that are very difficult to overcome. Black fathers are vowing to be good fathers because of attacks from society. This is easier said than done. Black men need to stop having children with women who never plan on marrying. One of my brothers had two children and luckily, they turned out ok but he never married their mother. I don't even know to this very day if he had any intention of marrying their mother. Another friend was married and we thought the marriage would last but he divorced his wife and never held another job where taxes would be taken out of his check. He didn't want to pay income taxes so he could avoid being tracked for child support. He had the children so he should have been man enough to support his children even if he wasn't married to their mother anymore. There are some child support dodgers and this happens in other ethnic groups, it isn't just black men who practice this behavior.

Change has been in the air and it has almost taken forty years to get here from forty years of inner-city pain and misery to determine the factors that have caused the highest statistics for single-parent homes in the black community. Families are so much stronger with two parents in the household with two good incomes. This is something that we all should aim for. Children can't control the behavior of adults and some children are caught in a mess that was created by their parents. The child isn't responsible for the behavior of their parents.

What I noticed about my cousins with two parents was that they seem to go on more trips. They always had the money for extra-curricular activities and some of their homes were more elaborate than what we had. They would always have new bicycles when I didn't have one. There was some jealousy that I do have to admit but I still played and did things with my cousins.

Comments: In all honesty, my belief in life is that all children should have two parents if that is possible in this world. Growing up in a family is one of the most positive experiences that a child can have. I could never comprehend why some women would have babies with different men without thinking about marrying these men. This is a mindset that I could never understand. Some mistakes can happen but when this pattern continues, something is going on that we just don't understand. When I was in public Education and I retired in 2016, I noticed that white women were becoming single parents and the kids that they had were from black men.

This became more prevalent in the late 2000s. We experience the same scenario when a lot of single black women were having kids with black men without being married. All children are entitled to two parents whether they are interracial or non-interracial. A home just doesn't seem complete without two parents. This is just my reality about society and how it should exist.

Chapter Six

The Art of Good Parenting

As the world continues to rotate on its axis, it is no big surprise that Black and White parents have a different approach to raising their children because they both come from different backgrounds. White children have the privilege of exploring the world differently which is demonstrated by running more freely in public places than some blacks. Black children are directed to accept the world of their parents above everything else and are taught to behave and be quiet in public places.

Some children are raised in a manner that shapes the way he/she sees the world. The way a child is disciplined and reared or lack of also determines how the world sees the child. Older Black parents and grandparents try to do their best to instill those children and grandchildren behave in public. This comes from the desire for Black children to be examined as non-threatening and more civilized in the public and the community. In reality, part of the reason Black parents are so tough on their children is that they don't want to perpetuate the Black stereotypes perpetuated by a racist society.

There was a study done by Parenting Styles African American and White Families with Children-Findings from Observational Study, research reveals that male children are parented more severely than their female counterparts in society. This might be an approach by some Black parents as an attempt to prepare their sons for the realities of White Supremacy. This kind of presenting might send the message that hostility, aggression, and violence are acceptable forms of behavior in communities.

There was a study done by The American Sociological Association in 2002 that indicates African American parents favor the disciplinarian or authoritarian approach to parenting. This study might be accurate because when we misbehaved, we were punished with switches or tree limbs as what they were referred to in the '70s in the black community. We were also disciplined with extension cords. I do recall an incident where my mother was furious with me because she sent me to the neighbor's house to ask the neighbor for some wax paper but she wanted aluminum foil. I didn't hear her correctly as to what she wanted me to get from the neighbor. I returned home with the wrong item. My mother was so upset with me. She went into her bedroom and retrieved an extension cord and proceeded to strike me with the extension cord. During the process, I kept trying to block the strikes against me with my hands and my face was had red impressions from the extension cord that hurt. She then had me go back to the neighbor's house with my face red with marks and ask for the right item that she requested. It was embarrassing to go back in that condition. My neighbor didn't ask any questions but she could see the marks on my face.

As we continue to examine the study mentioned above, the study involved 302 African American adolescents and their mothers, and the study revealed that Black parents developed a more take-charge philosophy to parenting than their white, middle-class counterparts. The study reiterates that Black parents tend to be harsher on their children as an attempt to prepare them for the real world that is filled with so much discrimination and societal biases that do not favor people of color and in 2021 still do not favor the Black Community.

There is another important component of Black parenting compared to white parenting. The American Sociological Association conducted another study that examines religion in the Black Community. Religion plays a vital role in the Black Community. The study reveals that regardless of social class, Black parents were more likely to send their children to Bible camp and Sunday School, while their white peers encourage their children to participate in activities such as piano lessons and soccer camp. This theory seems to hold because we were required to attend Sunday School every Sunday morning and we also had to attend Vacation Bible School every summer.

As we explore some practices of Black families in the past, these factors reveal that not a great deal has changed in terms of the values most African Americans hold dear in terms of child-rearing. It is important to remember raising children who are structured and hard-working is very important in society, regardless of ethnic background. The data stresses that a balance of discipline is necessary for most Black children.

We know how important it is to spend quality time with children, learning their interests, and enforcing chores and household duties while encouraging social time are remedies for Black parents to teach their children some values of respect and responsibility by encouraging healthy parent/child interaction and enhancing the child's social skills and work ethic. As parents enforce these ideals, this can help to ease some fear Black parents have about the destiny and fate of their children in the world. When Black parents promote a balanced approach to life, this can also increase the chances that the child will grow into a productive and well-rounded member of the community.

People understand and the primary goal for good parenting is to convey values, beliefs, and ideas around lifestyles based on cultural knowledge of adult tasks and competencies needed for proper functioning in our society. For African-American parents delivering an awareness of cultural values and norms is injected into parenting; reflecting on childrearing, it has been influenced by the dismantling of support systems through the experience of slavery and Jim Crow laws after the reconstruction period, and other forms of modern racism and aggression. We know that corporal punishment has been administered as a way of control and restrain behavior and youth. We need to try and fully understand the use of physical punishment in African-American families. We need to appreciate both historical and psychological factors that influence family dynamics.

Literature suggests that parenting styles, behaviors, characteristics, and strengths of African American families are guided by their cultural heritage and beliefs. African American families have flexible roles that allow for acceptance and change. Children are instructed to be obedient and respectful in the family setting and kinship settings when they deal with elders. The research on African-American parenting indicates that Afrocentric norms and values are very important in childrearing dynamics and attitudes. Black parents have always stressed cleanliness, family ties, independence, obedience, religion, and moral and personal values, such as behaving and respecting others as I indicated earlier.

As a child, my fear came in the form of physical punishment and I am sure that other children felt the same way as I did growing up in a very structured household in the early '70s and beyond. Physical punishment was incorporated into parenting expectations. Parents did use physical punishment to prevent certain behaviors from getting completely out-of-control that might lead to serious crimes later in life. African American parents tend to spank children to prevent embarrassment in public places than white parents.

During slavery, children were required to learn to obey to keep themselves out of trouble. Their identity is reflected in how they behaved on the plantation. Slave owners use physical punishment to control and reinforce obedience and was a way to keep children under control. The research also states that modern parents endorsed physical punishment as a method to decrease defiant or oppositional behavior, prevent children from endangering themselves, and eradicate continued disobedience with increased rates of spanking in low-income families. As I indicated before, African American mothers were reported engaging in more spanking and discipline resulted in more behavior problems down the road. As we examine the importance of education which is a strength of black families and how it can enhance potential economic benefits and security for families, leading to high expectations around grades. Growing up and receiving poor grades did lead to some kind of punishment. Black parents have felt compelled to use swift punishment to protect their children.

There are methods to reduce physical punishment in African-American families by better practices in parenting in general. Family practitioners need to support parenting approaches that draw on the strengths of the family dynamics and spirituality. The idea of respect for elders needs to be reinforced as important to help parents to deconstruct parenting goals based on their underlying values and goals can help redirect parents toward more positive parenting approaches.

We need in our communities' programs that include more racial socialization strategies, measures, and techniques to promote and demonstrate resiliency in our youth to assist them with developing a more positive racial identity. A positive self-concept and racial identity are more important in this world than anything else as we move into the next century. Racial socialization is vital to a society that has been such a challenge for African Americans. Self-esteem along with school efficacy and achievement is important to the development of the black family dynamics. Parents can be guided as to how to assist children with making positive self-statements and affirmations around identity, self-efficacy, and academic achievement. Parents should be encouraged to connect with other families, church, and community organizations to build support systems to encourage youth development and reduce parenting stress. Parents also should encourage their children to develop the skills to be bicultural by navigating both majority and minority cultures. Many measures can reduce the rates of physical punishment in African-American families by strengthening our communities.

Parenting is one of the most difficult challenges that adults have to face in this world. I have never been a parent and don't claim to be one. I do understand how hard it is and it is a very rigorous responsibility. It was obvious that my parents had some very challenging responsibilities for raising nine children. It seemed very exhausting because they had to feed and provide for nine children upon providing all of their needs. You also had to incorporate welfare in the trajectory. A family has many expenses.

There were some comments made about my parents and some of the choices that they made as I was growing up. These choices were questionable and some of them I didn't agree with. As I indicated, my mother was going with a married man while my father was still married to his wife. These circumstances didn't make them bad parents. We were surrounded by parents that cared for their children. Love was always a major function in our household. They always positively provided for the family even if our father lived in a different household. There was some envy of my cousins because they had both parents living in the same household and both parents had full-time jobs.

As we grew older, children start to become more challenging and start indulging in things that might get them in trouble with the law, etc. My father was an enabler for one of my brothers as he entered adulthood. Trouble tends to come knocking at your door when you least expect it. We didn't have any serious issues with the law growing up as kids. As a parent, you should establish rules for your children to adhere to. You shouldn't allow children to create the dynamics of your household. You need to be the best role model that you can be. You don't want your children picking up bad habits in the streets or picking up bad habits that they have inherited from the friends that they hang out with. These bad habits can land them in jail. You must become a moral compass for your children at a very early age. It is important to establish a positive foundation so children will have something to follow and respect. Your positive behavior is the key to your child's success in life.

It is very important to know who your kids hang around with growing up in elementary school, middle and high school. Get to know the parents of your children's friends. There are so many bad apples in the world and you want your children to stay away from them. Children are easily influenced by the people that they hang around with. Make sure that you know who they socialize with at school and when they aren't attending school. My parents allowed my brothers to hang around with children that were negative role models. These children's behavior was very questionable. I saw so many shady characters hanging around with my brothers growing up in high school. This time was at the height of the marijuana smoking era. My brothers were smoking pot when it was illegal. They continued to smoke marijuana and sell marijuana through high school.

Some parents act surprised when they receive a phone call from the police station. It is important to listen to your children and give them the proper attention so that they don't get this attention from friends and other people that they hang out with. Don't be afraid to ask questions if you think that something is wrong or you suspect that they might be doing something that might land them in jail or prison. It is hard to police your children twenty-four hours a day. You need to build trust in them so that they will never do something that you think is against their character as human beings. This doesn't mean that you have to be so strict and this does turn some children against their parents. The last thing that you want them to do is to start them hating and despising you because of the way that you treat them. You could be the best parent in the world and your child could still wind up having encounters with the law. A parent has to establish authority in the household right away with their children.

I can recall telling my parents when I was a teenager don't be so quick to believe everything that comes out of their mouths. My brothers told lies to my parents that I knew weren't the truth. Another point that I would like to make is: Don't be so quick to defend them and their conduct when you don't have all the facts. Some parents feel that their children can't do anything wrong in this world. They are delusional when they continue on this path. A child can make one mistake but if this child keeps making the same mistakes, this should be a red flag. I grew up in a different era but some of the same issues that we dealt with still exist today. As my brothers ventured into adulthood, some of them had minor encounters with the law. They needed help from my parents and what I found out was that my parents weren't getting the correct version of what caused them to bump heads with the police. Some of the things that my brothers told my parents weren't truthful and they knew that they weren't telling the truth. My information would come from reliable sources.

When children see things that their parents do in the household, they want to emulate these things even if they are bad. This would include things like smoking cigarettes, smoking pot, drinking alcohol, and other things that we might find inappropriate. These were activities that I never indulged in. Smoking marijuana does lead to an appetite for stronger drugs that might be illegal. This is what happened to one of my brothers, he started doing crack cocaine and to this very day, he has never been able to break the habit. He has had many encounters with the police but he was never locked up. One brother is still doing crack cocaine from the early seventies to the present.

We have seen how we are treated by cops and the killing of our people for years. We have lost many black lives to cops. We need to express how we want our children to deal with cops when they are pulled over or approached by a police officer so that our children will not wind up being killed. Make sure that you tell them not to escalate the situation and become hostile with a cop. Tell your children to listen to the cop and do what is asked of them so that the cop will not be angered. Police anger is what leads to the death of some people. Make sure that your children don't give them an excuse to use extensive force on them. You don't have to compromise your integrity. It is important to avoid any drastic action by cops that might leave you dead. Some of the cop's behavior is justifiable just as long as it doesn't land you in jail or being shot. Don't poison the mind of children with the idea that all cops are bad. Most cops feel humanity for mankind and people of color. All cops aren't out to destroy African Americans. There are a lot of good cops in this world and I have come across a lot of them during my lifetime. Bad cops do give the good cops a bad reputation because of their attitude against people of color.

Set an example each day for children to do what is right. You can alleviate some of the problems that they might have with cops in the future. Your example should start at a very early age especially in elementary school. Teach them the difference between what is wrong and what is right. I know that this might be a challenge for some parents but it can be done with a very positive attitude. When they have friends come over to visit, get to know these friends, and learn everything that you can about their family. Bad behavior is learned on the streets more so than in the household. Invest time with your children, listen to them, get to know them, and understand them. We should never let society be the mother and father of our children. Don't allow society to tell your story. You should be the author so that when you do tell it, it will be inspirational to the readers. This would raise your confidence to the highest level possible. We need to erase some of the stereotypes that have been plaguing African Americans for decades. It is up to you what life you chose whether you win or lose.

Comments: Raising a child today can be very challenging but don't let that put a damper on your chances of raising law-abiding citizens that will be productive in society. We have been experiencing so much unrest and the reality of police brutality and the development of the "Black Lives Matter Movement." We should never underestimate the value and rewards of being a good parent.

Chapter Seven

Nutrition and the African American Diet

Nutrition is vital in every lifestyle. Race doesn't distinguish the importance of living a healthier lifestyle. Growing up was somewhat a challenge because of being on welfare and Aid For Dependent Children. Welfare did supply food sources for black families that were on welfare. The food that was distributed was full of unhealthy choices such as starch, sugar, the saturated fat that was rated low on the nutritional scale. We were given free cheese, rice, macaroni, raisins, peanut butter, powdered eggs and some of these items did have some nutritional value. We never complained because we always had something to eat.

Some of my family members developed diabetes, hypertension, cancer, and other serious issues probably because of their diet and lack of exercise. Other relatives developed some of these physical ailments when I was growing up in Indiana. My parents, sisters, brothers, cousins, and other relatives drank a lot of alcohol and beer. This conduct probably led them to develop diabetes because beer is processed with high amounts of sugar for processing. My father was an alcoholic and my mother was somewhat of an alcoholic as well. My father developed diabetes at the age of forty-six and my mother was considered a borderline diabetic at the age of fifty. A sister started smoking cigarettes and indulging in alcohol at the age of fifteen when she moved to Chicago to stay with relatives. These activities just didn't seem to entice me at any level growing up in a houseful that involved themselves in drinking alcohol and other unethical substance abuse activities.

People were aware that cigarette smoking could cause cancer and serious health problems including doing damage to the lungs. This didn't seem to deter any of my family members. My mother smoked but was considered a light smoker. Some brothers and sisters smoked for years. This was a habit that was allowed in my household in Gary, Indiana. There were times when the second-hand smoke would bother me as I inhaled the smoke. The entire house would wreak of the smell of tobacco. Going to college was my escape and I couldn't wait until that occurred in 1977 when I graduated from high school. Bad habits of smoking were developed in high school by my brothers and sisters and other relatives. Everyone seemed to be smoking cigarettes in the early seventies and some of them are still smoking in 2021. People have disregarded the health issues and have wound up paying the price for bad habits that led to some serious diseases.

The African American diet has always been an issue for decades but given little attention growing up. It is very important to understand the African American Diet and how you can be healthier without completely straying away from your heritage when it comes to nutrition and adapting to a healthier lifestyle.

There have been some serious health issues associated with the Soul Food Diet. These were things that my mother and father weren't aware of. Nutrition didn't seem to be that important growing up. It was all about making sure that you had enough food to eat no matter what the source was even if it was handouts from welfare. Survival was a very important component of the Black community.

Our preferences for food developed from our culture as African Americans. The Soul Food Diet led to different health problems for African Americans. Our diet consisted of fried food and lots of fatty meats saturated in rich gravies that clog your arteries and led to health problems over years. This is what caused my father, mother, brothers, and sisters to develop heart problems. We associate the food with social awareness and the history of slavery. The effort to get us to eat healthier foods was met with resistance with the attempt to eliminate our black culture. This doesn't mean that we can't eat some foods associated with the soul food diet that might be healthier so that we can combat the higher rates of obesity that lead to cardiovascular disease.

Our social gatherings are centered around food events and even funerals. This originated in the South. My parents were from the South. Soul food is a cuisine that signifies the history of African Americans. It is a known fact that we still have some of the highest rates of obesity and heart disease because of our lifestyle for decades. So many of my relatives fell victims to high blood pressure, obesity, and other cardiovascular diseases for eating so much fried food. Some things can be done today to establish a healthier lifestyle with determination. This would include investing time in researching other healthier diets that might include becoming vegan etc. The diet industry has created so many options in the 21st Century. We need to encourage our people to develop healthier eating habits and this is something that I mentioned to my parents. The typical soul food diet isn't very healthy and some blacks have known this for many years. We don't have to give up our culture completely. We can make some positive changes and still enjoy eating some soul food.

We have to look at how culture affected the African-American diet. You can go back in history and examine some of the eating habits of African Americans in the United States. Culture fusion came from the English settlers, Native Americans, and African slaves that developed some of the basics of Southern cuisine. As you examine African-American History, the African slaves loved to fry, boil, and roast dishes using pork, pork fat, corn, sweet potatoes, and local green leafy vegetables which were used by the British, French Americans, and Spanish. We ate all these foods growing up because this is what my mother knew how to cook from her heritage. We also ate pig feet, ham hocks, hog head cheese, chitlins, hog mogs, and other African cuisines with a lot of fat. Fat does give flavor to so many foods. My mother would prepare leafy green vegetables such as turnip greens, collard greens, mustard greens, okra, black-eyed peas, pinto beans, sweet potatoes, and other things that were treats.

The things that we ate were mostly always fried. Watermelon was always eaten during the summer months. Lard was also used to fry certain meats. This substance has a very high-fat content. When you would visit the homes of African Americans, most of them had a can of grease on the stove for frying. The food that some of us continue to eat today was influenced by the dominant American culture. So many of us feel that by eating healthier, we are giving up the culture that was instilled in us by our parents and ancestors. This means giving up soul food. People think that it is an obligation to serve soul food to our guests at social gatherings because this is what blacks are accustomed to. So many of us are very reluctant to eat healthier foods because our friends and relatives might be insulted. Healthier food doesn't seem to have the same taste as food prepared in a lot of fat.

You can still cook vegetables with flavor by substituting turkey wings instead of using salt pork or ham hocks. Today, you can cook some of the same food but eliminating some fat.

Certain ethnic groups have a higher risk for certain diseases based on their diets, genetics, culture, and lifestyle. African Americans are plagued with heart disease and cancer because of their diet. They have a higher percentage of deaths compared to other ethnic groups. This would include hypertension and obesity also. Our main focus of the future should be to improve these conditions by adopting a healthier lifestyle through nutrition. It is a proven fact that the typical soul food diet involves large amounts of meat, fat, and sugar that leads to obesity, heart disease, and stroke. African Americans are choosing fried chicken, barbecued ribs, baked macaroni and cheese, sugary fruit drinks, sweet potato pie that is very typical of soul food meals. Exercise and diet are crucial. They play a major role in the survival of all African Americans. Other ethnic groups also have high occurrences of diabetes, hypertension, cancer, and heart disease when compared to the white population. It has been determined that 35 percent of all cancer deaths in the United States are attributable to diet. It is never too late to start thinking about living a healthier lifestyle.

One of the reasons that contribute to cancer is that fewer than one-quarter of adults consume the recommended five or more daily servings of fruits and vegetables. Some minorities consume less than that. This is why we have higher rates of cancer incidents in African-American Communities to this very day. There was a survey that was conducted and it found that 88 percent of African Americans didn't eat any dark green leafy vegetables, and about 94 percent had no deep yellow vegetables on any given day of the survey. So many people fall short of the necessary vitamins on the daily allowances chart for vitamin E, Vitamin B-6, calcium, magnesium, and zinc. The report also states that 35 percent of our calories came from fat and 12 percent from saturated fat. It is recommended by a Nutritionist that 30 percent or fewer calories come from fat and less than 10 percent from saturated fat. Blacks also have the highest obesity prevalence at 33.9 percent.

Exercise and diet have to play a major role in the lifespan of African Americans. Your life becomes so much easier when you are healthier human beings. I realized the importance of exercise as I got older and saw what the lack of exercise did to some of my family and relatives. People tend to look at exercise as a challenge. It is a serious challenge and it can lead to less stress and you feel so much better. This has been tested and found true. We come up with so many excuses as to why we shouldn't go to the gym or start an exercise regimen at home. It is so easy to grab a large piece of cake and a big bowl of vanilla ice cream instead of taking time to exercise. It is very important to prioritize in this life. Since I started seriously exercising in the early eighties to the present, I feel so much better and it is easier to deal with the challenges of the day. My outlook on life has improved substantially over the years because of exercise and choosing healthier food choices. Diabetes hasn't been an issue; high blood pressure or cancer hasn't come knocking at my door because of my positive lifestyle change. Exercising has become an activity in my daily routine.

We all know that some habits are hard to break and some lifestyle changes can be very difficult to accomplish. It is very hard to give up soda, sweets, etc. This can be nearly impossible to achieve.

We place ourselves in very serious health situations before we even start thinking about changing our diet or starting an exercising program. When my father had triple-bypass surgery that was a red light for me and a wake-up call to look at my lifestyle. Two of my brothers were diagnosed with congestive heart failure. They both have passed and another brother is still living with heart issues. I can't say this enough that it is never too late to change your diet and eat healthier. It does take willpower and determination but it can be done. You have to surround yourself with people that have the same beliefs as you do. This will help you achieve your goals in life that will eventually lead to a healthier lifestyle.

I can recall visiting some of my African-American friends in their homes and the homes reeked of the smell of grease and fried foods. There was a large can of grease on the stove. I have been very fortunate to realize some of the things that I have done wrong in life and start making some positive changes that will reflect my future. Attitude plays a vital role in just about everything that we do in life. If you want to stay or become healthier, you have to look at food differently than your parents when you were growing up. You wonder why your parents have heart attacks and strokes and ailing conditions as they age. These things probably developed because of their diets. Never go through life with the fear of taking chances. This will move you forward with a better outlook and a healthier lifestyle that you are entitled to. Please don't allow some of the ills of the past to be a reflection as to how you prevail in the future. Now, you have an awareness as to how to move forward that would include a healthier diet and exercise program after consulting with health professionals. It is very important to check with your doctor when you make lifestyle changes such as diet and exercise. There are guidelines that you should be aware of. We are seeing more Blacks considering becoming a vegan which might be healthier than our previous diet regiment.

There are so many healthier choices these days. The Internet has every kind of diet possible from meat-eaters to vegans, vegetarians, etc. Once you develop a different mindset, you are on the road to a better lifestyle. We have to examine some of the eating habits of our parents and ancestors and make better choices that include exercise and develop a positive attitude about wellness. I know that when my mother developed breast cancer, I thought that her diet had something to do with it. We did eat fried foods and consumed a lot of saturated fats, starch, and more sugar. The food that we ate was mostly given to us from Welfare which was cheap and food purchased in grocery stores. People just didn't think about eating in the terms of wellness in the early sixties and late seventies. It was about providing food for the family. As I got older, I realized that it was important for me to start exercising and obtaining a gym membership and that is what I did in the early eighties and have continued down that path to this very day in 2021. My entire attitude is different about food and how important my health is today. Sugar diabetes has been running rampant in my family. We can change those dynamics by adhering to a lifestyle change with our diet.

Some people can't afford gym memberships but there are some changes that you can make that don't cost that much money which includes walking, walking up and down stairs instead of always looking for the elevator. Park your car not so close to the entrance of a supermarket or other public buildings. People should try to move as much as possible.

Examining the Life Expectancy of Blacks

This has been a major issue for Blacks for many years acknowledging that we have been plagued with serious medical issues, poverty, racism, higher incarceration rates for black males, the Coronavirus, other hardships, etc., that have contributed to the decline in life expectancy for African Americans. Some black males have been known to avoid medical examinations and not take their health as seriously as black females. My mother passed away at the age of fifty-five years old from the complications of breast cancer. My father passed away from a series of minor strokes because of high blood pressure and diabetes at eighty-six. He never exercised or changed his high-fat saturated diet. He dealt with high blood pressure and diabetes for years. Two brothers passed away because of congestive heart failure before turning sixty-five years of age. Other relatives have had to deal with high blood pressure, diabetes, and other health issues that are prominent in the black community. This is why I have been stressing to people over the years, the importance of exercise and the proper diet for longevity in survival. There are better alternatives to improving your health beyond 2019.

The current data available in 2021, indicated the average life expectancy dropped by a year in 2020. This information was taken from the National Center For Health Statistics which is associated with the Centers For Disease Control and Prevention. It has been determined that the life expectancy at birth in the total U.S. population was 77.8 years which was a decline of one year from 78.8 in 2019. The life expectancy for males at birth was 75.1, a decline of 1.2 years from 78.8 in 2019. Female life expectancy declined to 80.5 years; a 0.9-year decrease from 2019. We all know that women tend to outlive men in black and white ratios. Women of all races seem to maintain an advantage in the life expectancy rate. We need to study women more and maybe this would give us a better understanding as to why their life expectancy seems to exceed other genders in both white and black communities.

Deaths from COVID-19 contributed to the decline in the United States life expectancy between January 2020 to the present according to the CDC. This disease has had such a very profound and devastating impact on African Americans as stated earlier and other people of color because of some of the underlying health issues that blacks have been facing for decades. Their refusal to take certain vaccines and the lack of trust in medical experts has been an issue along with Blacks being administered certain vaccines like the Coronavirus vaccine disproportionally compared to Whites. It has been a scary scenario with the Coronavirus.

The United States Life Expectancy Declined in 2020

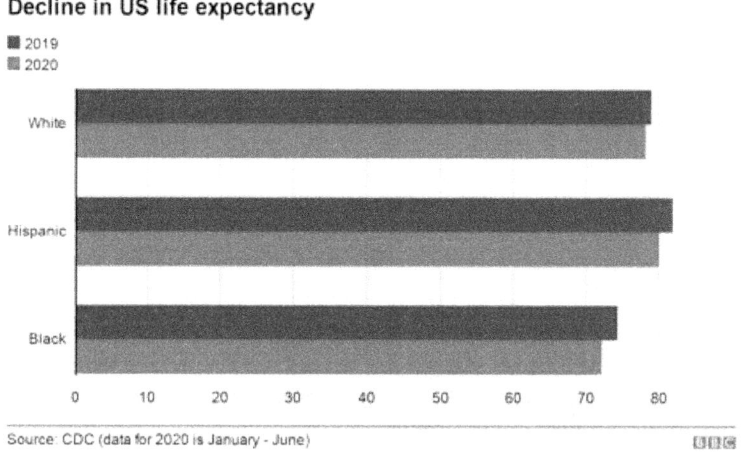

Before the Coronavirus hit America, there were slight drops in life expectancy due to the rise in overdose deaths according to NCHC spokesperson Jeff Lancashire. The COVID-19 Pandemic has been responsible for an estimated two-thirds of all excess death in 2020 and 2021.

It has been very obvious what groups have suffered the most decline in life expectancy because of the Coronavirus. The group that has had the largest decline in life expectancy was non-Hispanic Black males, their life expectancy dropped three years. We also know that Hispanic males also saw a large decline in life expectancy, a decline of 2.4 years. The data also shows that the non-Hispanic Black females saw a life expectancy decline of 2.3 years, and Hispanic females faced a decline of 1.1 years. Minority groups have always been the bearers of low life expectancy rates. As I stated, other factors that contributed to lower life expectancy are the environment that has fewer resources than some of the affluent communities where most whites live. This has been a disadvantage that affected so many black communities for so many decades. Our race has been a major factor in life expectancy. So many things affect our people, attitude and mindset is a contributing factor.

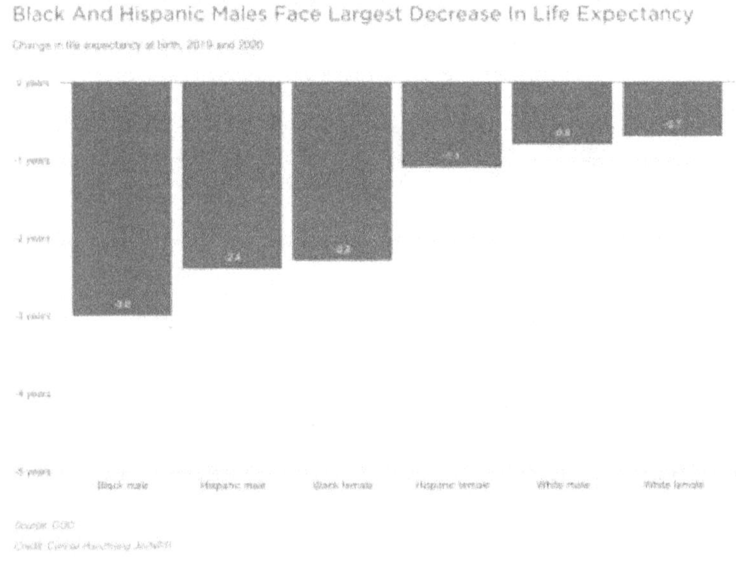

As I stated before throughout the coronavirus pandemic, Black and Latino Americans have died from COVID-19 at disproportionally higher rates. Some people couldn't understand their reluctance and hesitation for not wanting to take something that would probably save their lives. Reluctance to take the vaccine did lead to higher deaths in 2020 and beyond the period when the disease was very prominent in so many communities around the world. Education has helped and persuaded some Blacks to take this disease very seriously because of the impact that it had on communities of color.

When examining the life expectancy of Black men, the results are very disturbing. It is important to look at the Black men's health disparities. As we examine the life expectancy by race (Black: White inequities) and gender from 1900 to 2011. It has improved for all race/ethnicity and gender groups for the past 111 years. We continue to have a substantially lower life expectancy at birth than black women and white women and men. As we study the 1900s, the estimated life expectancy for white men was 46.6 years; non-White men was 43.5 years; for White women, it was 48.7 years; and for non-White women, it was 33.5 years. Moving to 2011, the life expectancy for White men was 76.6 years; Black men it was 72.2 years; White women it was 81.1 years; for Black women, it was 78.2 years.

The black male has been plagued by so many things in society. So many of them are incarcerated and this decreases their life expectancy. Their involvement in crime has also had a detrimental impact on the life expectancy rate. They seem to place their health on the backburner and don't consider it a priority as other races and even especially black women. It is so difficult being a black male in America considering all the circumstances stated above. We can change some of the dynamics with a different attitude and start prioritizing the things that are important to us. Our health should always be a number one priority.

When I think about some of the startling statistics, it reminds me of some of the behaviors that I watched throughout my life as my father, uncles, brothers, and cousins indulged in alcohol over the weekends as I was growing up. They looked forward to consuming alcohol starting on Friday and this behavior would last throughout the weekend. It was apparent to me that they didn't have any health concerns during this time. I can recall one cousin that would consume alcohol just about every day. He was so thirsty one day and they had to rush him into the hospital. He wound up having a stroke and was diagnosed with diabetes. He had no idea that he had diabetes until this was discovered at the hospital.

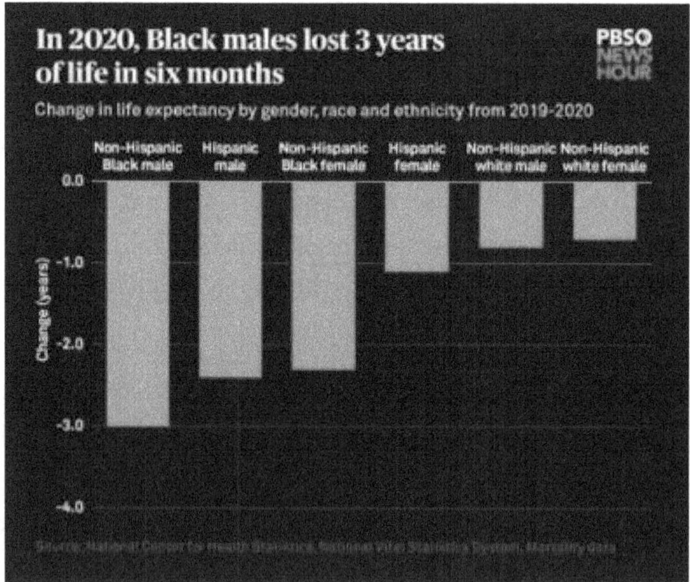

In 2013, the ratios remained consistent from birth to age seventy years (with Black male mortality rates about 40 percent higher than White male mortality rates) and then declined to 0

percent at age eighty-five years. We saw some improvement in life expectancy during the first half of the 20th Century because of the reduction in both infant and childhood mortality and reductions in rates from acute infectious diseases. Rates of decline were slower for Black men and women, resulting in larger relative ratios in life expectancy.

Efforts have failed in the health and well-being of black men when it comes to public health as a priority to eliminate racial and ethnic disparities that include interventions to improve men's health. Black men tend to neglect their health compared to Black women. They fare worse than Black women and White Americans in life expectancy, infant health outcomes, age-and-cause specific morbidity and mortality, insurance coverage, and access to adequate health care. Some of these inequities have been prevalent for many decades. We can change some of these outcomes with a better awareness of who we are and pursue knowledge that affects our well-being when it comes to health issues, financial issues, personal issues, diet, exercise, and mental illness, etc.

We need to understand that black men play a very important role during the formation of families. When we focus on reproductive health and preconception, these are potential points of intervention for acknowledging the health care needs of black men and their families. Men are very important to maternal and child health; they haven't played a significant role in current family health programs in the same manner as women. Black men are less likely than black women to receive preventive health services, have a regular source of care, or have health insurance.

We need to focus on instilling healthy habits and teaching young black males about the importance of self-maintenance is key to improving the overall health in black communities and the nation. It is important to provide boys and young men with the appropriate tools to maintain their health and for them to find a healthy balance between health, work, and family planning in preparing for fatherhood. The thing that I noticed about some men of color is that work is their number one priority which could lead to neglecting their health. If you aren't healthy, a job becomes useless and you might succumb to some kind of work termination because of bad health. This needs to change with a different attitude about the importance of maintaining good health.

Certain health agencies are looking at several conceptual frameworks that describe how the timing of social determinants and risk factors affect the health of black men and their families. As we look at future pathways of research success may depend on creating a men's health network that uses advances in computing and wearable technologies to gather data to build more knowledge with evidence-based strategies that address development disadvantages occurring in black men, with early interventions to address the social problems in childhood, in the adolescence of black men, and in early adulthood that can reduce illnesses in middle and late life, including other health factors that affect black men to eradicate disparities in their health and social issues. When we start addressing these issues, this will help to increase the life expectancy of black men and other ethnic groups.

We know that closing the racial gap in health will require improving African Americans' educations, employment, and income opportunities as well as creating environments that promote healthy behaviors such as a healthy diet, physical activity, and avoidance of tobacco, alcohol, and drugs. A four-year-old report from the Center on Society and Health published by the Virginia Commonwealth University looked at various zip codes around the world to examine the life expectancy of African American males and saw that life expectancy can differ by as many as twenty years between white and the majority of Black neighborhoods. Dr. Raynard Washington, The Department of Public Health's chief epidemiologist stated that in some ways, things are improving for Black men and boys, but there is still a gap between their health outcomes and others.

Comments: We know that there have been many issues that have contributed to the life expectancy of African Americans. We have been hearing these things for years. It is one thing to have these issues jumping up and down in our emotions. There are things that we can do by reading and investigating when we know that something isn't right when it comes to our well-being as humans even if it means comparing ourselves to other nationalities.

Chapter Eight

Black Voter Suppression (The 1800s-Present)

It is apparent that voter suppression has existed for decades before the Civil Rights Movement. It wasn't a fundamental right for people of color until 1965. Voting rights were a serious issue in the South. The Voting Rights Act of 1965 that was signed into law by President Lyndon B. Johnson was an attempt to overcome legal barriers at the state and local levels that prevented African Americans from exercising their right to vote as stated in the 15th Amendment of the United States Constitution. The Voting Rights Act is still considered one of the most far-reaching components of Civil Rights Legislation in the United States to this very day because of the impact that it had on the voting rights of African Americans.

As we moved ahead to the 2016 presidential election, voter suppression was still a major issue in the United States when it comes to Blacks exercising their constitutional right of voting in the United States. We know that voter suppression did help Donald J. Trump win in 2016 and it almost put him over the threshold to win the 2020 election. States have created racially biased election laws in battleground states imposing voter-ID legislation that favored Republican candidates. When former President Donald J. Trump lost in 2020, states are still trying to initiate and pass more laws restricting and making it harder for African Americans to vote in a majority of states where Republicans lose. People realized and anticipated that this would have a profound impact on the 2022 Midterm Elections to favor Republican candidates. This has always been their plan and scheme.

When they lose, this is attributed to the high turnout of Black voters especially in Georgia, Florida, Texas, New York, California, North Carolina, Illinois, Maryland, Virginia and Ohio, and other states where black turnout is very high. We have more voter suppression laws since Reconstruction. The Republicans are working quickly to restrict Blacks from voting in 2022.

There was a new poll conducted in 2018 by The Public Religion Research Institute (PRRI) and *The Atlantic* that discovered evidence of discrepancies in the ballots for Black and Latino voters, during the 2016 Presidential Election. We are going back to the Jim Crow Era of voting that created disenfranchisement of Blacks and Latino voters in America. We all thought that voting was a part of the American Dream as compared to White Americans. This hasn't been the case in the presidential elections of 2016 and 2020. There have been serious problems with voting irregularities of Blacks since the Reconstruction Era in the South.

We know for a fact that voter suppression in the United States is highly contested by African Americans and other people of color. As we examine the poll taxes and literacy tests of the past, we have experienced restrictive election laws that are frequent and racially neutral, making them almost legal. The data suggests that these laws and outcomes are nowhere racially neutral. This poll was conducted in June of 2018. The poll surveyed Americans about their experiences with voting, their interpretation of the country's political system. The outcome was very disturbing. They discovered that voter suppression was evident in 2020 and beyond and that voting is routinely more difficult for people of color than for their white counterparts in the United States according to the data.

The new data for voter suppression is alarming and paints a terrible scenario of opponents on their goal of restrictive voting laws. In the 2016 election, 9 percent of Hispanic respondents said that they experienced some voter suppression and someone in their household and were told they didn't have the proper identification to vote, while 3 percent of whites said the same. Ten percent of Blacks and 11 percent of Hispanics were told that they weren't listed on the voter rolls as compared to 5 percent of white respondents. Blacks have always noticed the discrepancies when it comes to voting and this continues to happen beyond 2022.

Voter suppression has become a contagious disease for people of color as we continue to exercise our right to vote in 2020 through the present. Sixty-eight percent of black respondents expressed that disenfranchisement is a major problem for Black Americans voting in the Land of the Free. The data suggests that disenfranchisement is the biggest challenge that we are still facing today. It has become an electoral problem in America for decades. How could something be so important to people and America become so restrictive? As we continue to jump over hurdles and the evils that have plagued the Black Community, we know that there is still some hope in humanity and mankind. The world is so off-balanced but things can change when we elect representatives that are sensitive to the issues that have affected people of color for decades. It has been very hard for Blacks to feel optimistic about voting of the continued efforts of Republicans to try and prevent and invalidate the votes of African Americans. The Republicans will continue to suppress in elections where the fear of losing is a serious threat and I know that voter suppression will occur in the 2022 midterm elections. As we look at the issue of voter suppression, there is a big difference in race and ethnicity when it comes to voting and the electoral system. When whites are asked about disenfranchisement, only 27 percent indicate that eligible voters are being denied the right to vote at the polls. They don't think it is a major problem. Many blacks don't feel that way.

The data also indicated that about six out of ten Blacks and Hispanics think that it is a problem. In the 2020 election, Stacey Abrams orchestrated and organized a very strong and positive campaign registering many Blacks in Georgia to vote in the 2020 Presidential Election. Her efforts with the assistance of others were very successful and President Biden won the state of Georgia along with Democrats getting control of the United States Senate. Georgia is turning into a Blue State. The Democrats won in the other Red States because of the efforts of many

Black voters. Now, states are imposing new voter laws to try to restrict and make it harder for Blacks to vote because of Democratic wins in Wisconsin, Pennsylvania, Arizona, Georgia, Michigan, and other states of the Union. As we move beyond 2020, Republicans will continue on their tirade to impose voter suppression and other tactics to disenfranchise voting for Blacks and people of color. This is because they lost the presidential election in 2020 and senate seats. They will move fiercely to enact hundreds of laws restricting voting for Blacks and voter inequality in 2022 and beyond. We all know that blacks couldn't vote until 1965. We were still faced with voting challenges in 2021. You would have thought that America has learned from the dark shadows and evils of the past. This is not the case because Republicans continue to try to impose laws that restrict Blacks from voting. They were all excited about voting by mail until they started losing in states.

It is a known fact that everyone should be entitled to exercise their 15th Amendment to vote in America. Heading to 2022 and beyond, Blacks will continue to face some serious voting hurdles. We know that we couldn't vote until 1965. There will be more challenges of voter suppression as we continue to have elections in the United States.

Voter suppression has become a major weapon for the Republican party especially when they started losing the Red States along with changes in the Postal Service slowing down the mail during the 2020 election. Some drastic changes were imposed by the Postmaster General of the United States. Staffing hours were cut, mail processing machines were removed from post offices in the United States. Maildrop boxes were removed in certain communities in the United States especially in Black Communities. These were serious challenges in my black communities and none of these changes were needed in any Black Communities. Some of these changes did create a very negative effect on mail delivery and mail-in ballots that didn't make it to the post office before the deadline. We know that these changes were instituted by the Postmaster General to prevent momentum by the Democratic Party to win the 2020 Presidential Election. So many of these tactics backfired because the Democrats won the presidency. The mail-in ballots increased for Blacks in 2020.

The Republican Party is living in fear because Non-Hispanic white people are becoming a shrinking percentage of the United States population and won't be a majority within a few decades. The Republican Party finds this troubling for their party and this is an indication that beyond 2022, it is going to be very challenging for them to maintain control of the House and Senate and even the White House in future presidential elections. They have been able to maintain political power, wealth disproportionately through discriminatory tactics that go back hundreds of years. Their power was threatened in 2020 by demographic shifts and backlash because of an unpopular president. Their effort to rule from the minority for such a long time to the present has become more desperate and more severe. Slowing down the mail and speeding up Supreme Court appointments was obvious during the reign of the 2016 president of the United States.

Other tactics that have been created by Republicans to stay in power in 2020 were: shutting down polling places in Black

Communities, opening more white ones, stopping the counting people of color in the 2020 Census so they would have less representation in Congress and fewer federal dollars invested in their communities and districts, stopping the counting the ballots where Blacks have voted, this tactic has worked before, prohibiting government agencies and schools from talking about the parts of the United States history that reveal the track record and rationale behind these maneuvers.

Republican legislatures and governors creatively blocked African Americans, Hispanics, and Asian Americans from the polls in previous elections in fear of the imminent demographic collapse of the Republican Party where their overpowering white constituency is becoming smaller of the electorate because of their inability to create policies that address and speak to a growing diverse nation. They would rather disenfranchise instead of reform.

In the 2020 election for Donald Trump, the goal of the Republicans was to target Black voters not to convince them to support Trump which everyone thought was a useless cause in some cases. They wanted to discourage Blacks from voting at all. They knew that most Blacks didn't support Trump in the first place. He had the lowest support of Black votes than any other president in the history of voting. These are the many examples that have been lurking in the shadows to discourage Blacks from voting in decades and during the Jim Crow Era. You would have thought that they would have learned something about their tactics.

Other issues affected the well-being of Blacks and people of color but that would have to come in another book. We need to remember Black Voter Suppression existed in the early 1800s and spilled into the 2000s. It seems to be more prevalent now than ever before in history. Slaves were not allowed to vote because they weren't even considered decent human beings. States have also been trying to prevent felons from voting especially in Florida. This has sparked concern from Democratic lawmakers.

We will never forget the 2020 President Election and experienced the scheme of voter suppression so that Trump would win another term. The Republicans waged an unrelenting attack on mail-in-voting which sent Biden over the top and in the lead as they continued to count these votes. When mail-in-voting worked for the Republicans in past elections, it wasn't an issue. Comments were made by the Trump Administration that mail-in-ballots will lead to massive fraud and a rigged election. It was obvious that early voting and voting by mail did reduce the advantage that Republicans might have had leading up to the 2020 election. There were many deterrents that Republicans thought would keep black voters from the polls especially with the Coronavirus running rampant in so many communities around the world. This didn't deter black voters because they stood in line for hours through rain and whatever the weather was to cast their vote as the Coronavirus was still an issue.

Even though Trump lost the 2020 election fair and square he and the Republicans are perpetuating the falsehood that the election was stolen from Donald Trump and the majority of his supporters support that theory in 2020. Trump filed many lawsuits for voter fraud and lost just about every one of them. The Secretaries of State in just about all the states indicated that the 2020 election was one of the fairest elections in the history of voting.

Comments: The focus of this section was to focus on what is happening in Black Communities today when it comes to voter suppression which has been a contagious disease for Blacks and other people of color. It existed in the early 1800s and during slavery.

Black Stereotypes of the Past and Present

Stereotypes have always been something that I find disturbing especially when it is directed at a certain nationality or a group of people. This would include stereotypes about Blacks, Whites, Asians, Latinos, etc. Some of the stereotypes developed before and during the time of enslavement of blacks. As an African American, I became aware of them as a child growing up in a Midwestern City. My parents were born in the South and when they moved to the North, these stereotypes came with them. My parents never talked about some of the stereotypes of the South and they never made negative comments about whites.

During the development of motion pictures and in the early 1920s, you could examine some of the images portrayed by black actors and black actresses in the black and white film era. Some blacks were cast as maids and butlers. Some of the early actors like Sidney Poitier played more serious roles on the screen. Actresses like Dorothy Dandridge, Ruby Dee, Josephine Baker, Eartha Kitt, Lena Horne, and others didn't play maids like Hattie McDaniel, Butterfly McQueen, and some of the other actresses. Some of these actors were only given certain domestic roles that we would find offensive today. Some of the black actresses were typecast only to certain roles as well as some of the black actors of the era. We eventually experienced better portrayals of black actresses like Diahann Carroll, Pam Grier, Rosalind Cash, Diana Sands, Vonetta McGee, Brenda Sykes, and Denise Nicholas and there were many more in the early seventies. The film industry was booming and blacks had positive roles.

It was kind of difficult for Blacks to obtain decent roles in the early 1920s through 1960s. As we moved into the 1970s and beyond, better opportunities started to appear in the likes of Viola Davis, Angela Bassett, Halle Berry, Diana Ross, Denzel Washington, Eddie Murphy, LaVar Burton many others. We know that Sidney Poitier had a very illustrious career in Hollywood for many decades. His career took off in the early 1940s through 2008. One of my favorite movies done by him is *In the Heat of the Night* and I can think of many others that were a standout. He has been nominated many times for an Oscar and he has won one. I was drawn to movies by his talent. He set the bar so high for other actors and actresses that came after him. The roles that he played allowed Americans to see positive images of Blacks on the big screen. I can remember seeing some pretty good movies with Blacks during the late seventies. Some of my favorite movies were *Sounder* and *Lady Sings the Blues*.

Other stereotypes that have been perpetuated over the years about blacks are: most Blacks are on welfare, Blacks have lower IQs than other races, they don't have strong work ethics, they sell drugs, they steal, they can't be trusted, they are porch monkeys, they are referred to as Bees, etc., and the list goes on. Some of these stereotypes can be associated with bad choices and bad behavior that I discussed in another chapter of this book. These behaviors have been witnessed by whites and other ethnic groups. You might be able to link certain conduct as a stereotype if it is repeated constantly. I am not indicating that there is a standard for assigning stereotypes. One stereotype that has been going for years is that black males have larger dingdongs than white males, a stereotype that was created by the Mandingo image during slavery. As a black man, this stereotype might be true but I am not going to subject myself to giving a response to that stereotype.

Certain conduct by blacks initiated some stereotypes. I am not indicating that there is a standard for assigning stereotypes. stereotype. A very good friend of mine went out with a white guy and she referred to his anatomy. She said to him during an intimate moment: “Does that come in an adult size?” It was kind of funny when she made that comment and I didn’t respond. I told her, “How could you say that to your date? I am sure he was embarrassed.”

Looking back in history, some of the early stereotypes of blacks evolved as a natural result of scientific racism and legal challenges of their humanity and citizenship as human beings. There was a Supreme Court case in 1857, Dred Scott vs. John F.A. Sanford, Chief Justice Roger B. Taney discharged the humanness of people of African descent. This legal paradigm permitted the image of African Americans to be diminished to caricatures in popular culture. There have been decades of old stereotypes and current-day incarnations of African American stereotypes such as Mammy, Mandingo, Sapphire, Uncle Tom, watermelon, which have been alerted by the legal and social status of African Americans.

So many of these stereotypes were created during the trans-Atlantic Slave Trade and were used to help to define black bodies and justify the business of slavery and other abusive attacks against Blacks. They could never classify an enslaved person as lazy because slaves worked diligently from sunrise to sunset. They worked under the violence against them. Slaves were accused of being submissive, backward, lewd, lazy, dishonest, and disloyal. Historically, these stereotypes were assigned to African Americans. If I had been a slave, I can imagine the kind of attitude that I would have projected being mistreated, beaten, and treated horribly. That lifestyle was so severe that it would send people into mental illness.

The Mammy stereotype has plagued the Black Community for decades. When you see a very big black woman, some people would refer to her as Mammy. This caricature developed during slavery also was popularized through minstrel shows. I did hear the word Mammy in my eighth grade Social Studies class and found the word offensive and insensitive.

Enslaved black women who were skilled in domestic work, worked tirelessly in the homes of white families and were caretakers for their children. These slaves were loyal servants to their slaveholders. Slaveholders made attempts to legalize the institution of slavery. The Mammy stereotype escalated after the Civil War and into the 1900s. The Pearl Milling Company became famous with the development of Aunt Jemima products which became synonymous with the Mammy stereotype. They even hired a real-life cook by the name of Nancy Green in 1899, to portray the character at the state and world fairs. As racial equality emerged in the last decades, in 2020, The Pearl Milling Company pulled back on some of these stereotypes by removing the words, Aunt Jemima from their products along with removing the image of an overweight black woman with a scarf on her head. This issue was very insensitive to African Americans for decades which carried many racial tones in the history of African Americans. The stereotype of an overweight, self-sacrificing dependent black woman figure grew with the American film industry through films *Birth of a Nation* (1915), *Imitation of Life* (1934), and *Gone with the Wind* (1939).

Uncle Tom

This is the name that has been used throughout history to describe a large broad-chested, powerfully made man of African heritage as described in the book by Harriet Beecher Stowe in 1852 in the novel, *Uncle Tom's Cabin*. Uncle Tom was a character that was described as submissive and obedient and he strived for white acceptance and approval by any means necessary. He was willing to give up his life to ensure the freedom of other slaves in the story. The term Uncle Tom became popular during the Great Migration when so many blacks felt the desire to move to Northern cities like New York, Chicago, and Detroit.

They wanted to escape the Jim Crow environments in the South. The Uncle Tom stereotype was recorded in a speech by Marcus Garvey in 1919. I have known many blacks to use the name "Uncle Tom" to refer to certain blacks in anger not knowing and understanding the history of this derogatory phrase. Knowledge is power. My parents participated in the Great Migration because they wanted to distance themselves from the evils and racism of the South and they sought out job opportunities to raise their family by going North.

Sapphire

This is another caricature that referred to a sassy black woman, emasculating and domineering in the 1800s through the mid-1900s. This concluded that African Americans were aggressive, loud, and angry in violation of social norms. The Sapphire stereotype gained its name on the CBS show *Amos 'N' Andy* about the character Sapphire Stevens. The show aired from 1951 to 1953 with an all-black cast. Sapphire Stevens had a husband on the show and his name was George "Kingfish" Stevens. He was described on the show as being ignorant and lazy. This Sapphire stereotype was new to me because I wasn't born around that time. My parents never mention that program as I grew up.

Watermelon

My parents loved watermelon, cantaloupe, honey melon because they grew up in the South and their parents grew these fruits. Amazingly, eating watermelon became a stereotype for African Americans in the South. Because of such a racial stereotype in the Jim Crow Era, watermelon once embodied self-sufficiency among African Americans. After the Emancipation, many Southern Africans would grow and sell watermelon as a symbol of freedom.

Many Southern whites turned the fruit into a symbol of poverty. Eating watermelon became a symbol of "unclean, lazy and childlike." Whites in the South would try to shame black watermelon merchants for selling such a fruit. In some aspects of history selling watermelon was income for some Southern blacks. Whites also found it strange for some blacks to eat watermelon without utensils and said it created a mess when eating it.

Mandingo (The Black Buck)

During slavery auctions, auctioneers were looking for black male slaves that promoted strength, breeding, ability, muscular strength, the Mandingo stereotype was born. While under the violence of enslavement, these physically powerful black men were thrashed and brutally forced into labor against their will and dignity as human beings. There was this myth and fear that these men would indulge in sexual revenge against white men through their daughters as displayed in the movie *Birth of a Nation* (1915). This stereotype of the Mandingo was animalistic and brutal which led to white mobs and militias that tortured and killed black men for the safety of the public during slavery. The Mandingos were accused of insulting and assaulting white women. These are many of the stereotypes that we have been faced with since slavery and many of them still haunt our conscience in modern culture. One stereotype that re-surfaced again since the early '60s is the phrase "Porch Monkeys" that came from seeing blacks during the summer months sitting on their porches in black communities, hanging out, and drinking lemonade.

Comments: It is disturbing that people would create stereotypes about people. Whites created these offensive comments about Blacks at the beginning of slavery in the United States that are still part of the trajectory of African Americans. The thing that I find upsetting is when we use these stereotypes on each other and don't find them offensive but if a white person refers to another black person with the same stereotypes, we want to retaliate immediately. I have experienced my people using the "N" word on each other and it isn't an issue. The word is deplorable and shouldn't be used by anyone. All races and ethnic groups tend to apply stereotypes to other ethnic groups and that doesn't make this issue right.

Chapter Nine

The Impact of the Coronavirus (2019-Present)

When I started writing this book, it was the height of the COVID-19 Pandemic. Who would have thought that the impact of this virus would have such a negative impact on the African American community and other people of color? It has been devastating to our people and has affected blacks more disproportionally compared to whites. Why do things of this nature have to have such a negative impact on the black community as compared to other ethnic groups? As we pursue this topic, I will reveal why we have been so prone to contracting this disease. Some things are beyond our control and that would include this coronavirus. Other things are due to the environmental, economic, and political factors that have existed for generations placing us at risk of chronic conditions that leave the lungs weak and immune systems compromised. We are more susceptible to asthma, heart disease, hypertension, and diabetes. This virus has attacked the compromised immune system of many African Americans. Some heredity factors couldn't have been altered in advance before this virus hit the United States attacking the most vulnerable population. It would seem that we have been the most vulnerable population when you examine the rate of transmission and deaths by this virus.

Reading the paper and watching the news, it has been devastating to see the impact of this virus on the black community. We account for 25 percent of those who have tested positive and 39 percent of COVID-related deaths compared to making up just 15 percent of the general population. This is a shocking analysis of how this virus has affected African Americans since the beginning of the virus in 2019. *The New York Times* stated that Black people account for more than half of those who tested positive in Chicago and 72 percent of the COVID-related deaths while making up less than a third of the population. When you look at the state of Illinois, Black people account for 25 percent of the COVID-related deaths while making up just 15 percent of the general population. You were seeing the same percentage in other states in the United States when you compare the same statistics to whites testing positive for the virus. Mayor Lori Lightfoot of Chicago has been on CNN, MSNBC expressing the severity of this virus when it attacked the residents in Chicago.

Michigan is another state where the virus has had a profound effect on the Black population. They accounted for 40 percent of the COVID-related deaths and just 14 percent of the population. In New Orleans, Black people accounted for almost 60 percent of the COVID-related deaths while making up less than a third of the population. We were dying at an astronomical rate that is twenty-five to thirty times higher than other ethnic groups. In 2020, the national mortality rate for Black was 23 deaths per 100,000 residents. In some states and Washington, D.C., mortality rates surpassed the national rate, In New York: 88 deaths (per 100,000 residents): Michigan: 72; Connecticut: 58; Louisiana; 49; New Jersey: 32; Illinois: 30: Washington, D.C. 27.

Blacks felt like this was some kind of horror movie because of the impact this virus had on us. We have been hoping that this nightmare would come to an end with the development of vaccines that have been very promising before the end of 2021. We knew that a lot of Blacks are homeless which makes them a higher risk for contracting the virus. We also are prone to having the lowest life expectancy rate compared to other communities. We experienced unequal healthcare treatment as compared to Whites. We are undertreated by some doctors because it is assumed that we have higher pain tolerance. Our medical needs have been underestimated by the medical profession which doesn't work in our favor to obtain decent medical assistance especially at the height of the COVID-19 pandemic in 2020.

Black business owners have suffered because of the COVID-19 pandemic. White families have ten times the amount of wealth as the median Black family according to the Brooking Institution. This comes down to Black Businesses having fewer reserves for financial and operational stability than white-owned businesses. The negative perception of Black-owned businesses in neighborhoods caused low investments due to racial and socioeconomic factors. The pandemic created this reality for blacks.

Social distancing harmed black businesses and the professionals who worked for them. Black businesses didn't receive the needed resources to protect themselves and serve their communities in the form of personal protective equipment afforded to White-owned businesses. The Cares Act did offer some relief to small businesses when it was available during the first Stimulus Legislation from Congress in 2020. Some black-owned businesses did apply in time and the money ran out before they could qualify. Congress was working on another Stimulus Package for small business owners but it stalled in Congress at the end of 2020. Hopefully, when this book is published, the black-owned business will have received more assistance without losing their businesses. Blacks were able to apply for loans during the American Rescues Plan in 2021. This helped some black businesses.

The Black community has never given up even when the odds have been against them during the height of the COVID-19 pandemic. The COVID-19 pandemic did cause some serious problems for them trying to maintain their businesses. We have been resilient during this entire ordeal that has affected our lives so drastically. Our strength has always come from the struggles that our ancestors have had to endure because of slavery and other ills of society that have been a detriment to our growth as human beings. Perseverance and determination have always been a part of our DNA. We do need the support of our elected officials at the federal, state, and local levels of government that are backed with concrete action when times are too hard to bear because of the impact of the virus in the United States.

The COVID-19 virus hasn't been an equal opportunity virus because it has affected Blacks so disproportionally than any other ethnic group. Inequality has always been an issue in the Black Community whether we like it or not. It is important to call on our leaders in Congress. As we look ahead to the future, we hope that one day the COVID-19 pandemic will be water under the bridge and we can move forward with a positive attitude. Vaccines were developed at the end of 2019 and these vaccines have been very helpful in trying to prevent the continued spread of the virus. 2021 is looking better with more people taking the different versions of the Coronavirus vaccines.

As an African American, I am yearning for the day when we aren't impacted by so many evil things that continue to be a part of our society and this would also help other ethnic groups as well. The cases for Blacks have risen substantially and homicides are just adding to the problem.

COVID-19 Vaccines and People of Color

Vaccines started to turn up at the height of the pandemic around 2019 and leading into 2020 and beyond. Pharmaceutical companies had been working diligently to create a vaccine that could be administered to slow the progression of the virus. Pfizer was one of the first companies to develop a very effective vaccine that has been administered to millions in the United States. It has been proven to be very effective after many trials and test runs. Moderna has also developed a vaccine along with Johnson and Johnson. Johnson and Johnson's vaccine could be administered with just one dose and Moderna and Pfizer require two doses that have been very good in preventing people from contracting the virus in 2021.

People of color have had many concerns at the onset of these vaccines. Their concerns focused on safety and effectiveness. It is a known fact that Black, Hispanic, Native American, and other people of color are overrepresented in the severe coronavirus disease that makes them more susceptible to the virus because of health issues that have plagued their communities for decades. These health concerns are diabetes and other health issues.

It is a fact the people of color, along with immigrants and differently-abled men and women have endured centuries of having their trust violated. The CDC has been trying to educate and give people facts about the vaccine's safety and efficacy, and renew trust toward health care in general. Health care organizers and leaders have tried to repair and restore trust in taking these vaccines. Health care organizations have been trying to rebuild confidence in the black communities by working strategically with local elected officials, community leaders, and religious leaders to convey accurate and essential health messages, including information about all the available vaccines. Blacks seem to trust their church more than medical professionals. Black ministers have a very positive effect on Blacks.

Blacks have been plagued with Institutional racism and historical inequities in health care may also play a role in vaccine hesitancy among African Americans and other people of color. Other incidents of the medical establishment endangering the health or betraying the trust of Black patients and research participants have complicated the relationship between the medical establishment and these communities. There is also a problem with a historical lack of diversity among health care practitioners and standard services and care afforded to patients living with poverty can create never-ending negative experiences with medical care. I know that we have to try and learn more about the vaccines and remember that knowledge is power and this would lead to concrete decisions about our health and welfare.

Chapter Ten

Law Enforcement (The Police) and Blacks

This is a very touchy subject because communities need the police. They are crucial and very important to all communities. This world would be in total disarray if there weren't any police bringing law and order to our society. One of the main responsibilities is to protect and serve and try to de-escalate serious situations that might lead to death. They are supposed to approach situations with a serious attitude of combatting violence and other criminal issues. All citizens should be treated in the same manner no matter what the circumstances entail. This would include white, black, and other people of color. We hope that there is no prejudice against anyone and at times, this isn't always the case.

You would think after the murders by police of African Americans, some of them would have a different attitude. I know that they should protect themselves when their lives are threatened and they are placed in harms-way. This doesn't mean being soft on crime but each situation should be approached professionally. The killing of blacks seems to be a very serious issue in the last five to ten years. With the unrest that police brutality has caused you would think that police would approach some of the encounters with blacks in a manner that would save their lives instead of causing death or serious bodily harm. Instead of shooting them point blank, when running, couldn't they shoot the victim in the leg to stop him? If they start running, let them run and make another attempt to track them down by the driver's license, etc. What techniques can they administer without bringing harm to themselves but allow the victim to live? These are my opinions about some of the encounters that I have seen on television that led to the development of the "Black Lives Matter" movement during the deaths of some African Americans in 2010 to the present. Why allow this behavior to destroy families and cities around the world?

This is a subject (The Police) that we dread discussing because they have been in the spotlight because of the deaths of blacks in Georgia, Minneapolis, Detroit, Wisconsin, and other areas in the United States. These deaths have led to riots, violence, and protests because of the killing of black men by police. This has been the focus when deaths by cops entered our radar from 2015 to the present. We are concerned about the lives of Blacks.

When you read the newspapers and watch the news, you would assume that all Blacks hate cops. Some cops have given blacks reasons to hate them. This isn't the case for all blacks. I understand the frustration with the police. Police have given Blacks reasons not to like them or question their judgment when administering law enforcement or when they have killed another black male. There is some fear about cops in general. We were afraid of the cops growing up in Gary. As I indicated in one of my other chapters about the ramifications of living near a low-income housing unit in the early '70s. I thought violence wasn't as prevalent during the early '70s as it is today in the 2000s. Many blacks have been murdered by cops in certain cities in the United States.

We know that cops are supposed to protect communities and serve as role models for justice in society. We rely on them to protect our communities without any kind of discrimination. People do unlawful things to provoke the police. I can recall an incident that I was involved in growing up and during this time, I was in the fifth grade. We were hanging out at night near the Projects mentioned in another Chapter, someone threw a rock and knocked out the streetlight. The police were called by one of the residents in the Projects. When the police came, we scattered and ran in fear. My brother and I ran and the cop chased us in pursuit. We were scared to death. We could have easily run home but we passed our home and ran in the alley behind our home. We hid underneath a car. For some reason, the cop knew that we were under the car. He started to kick underneath the car and bruised my brother's leg. We came out from under the car and the officer addressed the situation about the streetlight being destroyed. We informed him that we had nothing to do with the incident.

The officer lectured us about destroying property. He didn't take us down to the police station. When we got home, we explained to our mother what had transpired with the police. My mother was upset that my brother had a bruise on his leg. She went down to the Police Department to talk to the cop that bruised my brother's leg. She was very upset and she made it clear that what he did was wrong but she didn't file a complaint. Ironically, she knew the cop that kicked my brother. She said this was inappropriate kicking under a car and not knowing what you were kicking. This was the first encounter that I ever had with the police. This incident was a wake-up call for me at such an early age.

There are some bad cops and some good cops. I would say that most of them positively serve communities. Some of them are given a bad rap because of the bad cops. Some of them have stopped me from speeding and I wasn't given a ticket. All cops don't dislike blacks but some of them do. This is a reality that we can't ignore no matter how much we try. There is some good and bad in just about everything. The good always seems to overrule the bad things in society. This doesn't give me the reason to hate all cops. I try to avoid situations where I have to encounter cops.

When I was teaching in an all-white district, there were some issues with the white cops issuing tickets to blacks more so than whites. I was stopped in this area for a moving violation in 2013. A cop stopped me and I told him that I didn't see the sign that said: "No Left Turn at the Light." He checked my driving record and saw that I didn't have any tickets.

There weren't any points that I accumulated on my license. My driving record was excellent. This cop was shocked that this black man didn't have any points on his license. This area was known for stopping more African Americans for violations in comparison to white citizens. In hindsight, I thought that he wasn't going to give me a ticket because of my clean record. I was wrong and he did issue me a ticket. He knew that I was a teacher teaching at the local public school in Gary. Three points were added to my record which stayed on my record for three years. When stopped, I didn't get hostile or cause any issues for him.

There is no doubt that you might run into some bad cops and you will run into some good cops also. This is a reality that we don't have any control over. For some strange reason, I thought that I was given a ticket because of my race and I was in an area that targeted blacks for speeding and other traffic violations. Please don't judge bad apples with good apples. We live in a society where people like some people and hate other people. All white cops aren't racists but some of them are. Some black men seem to be targets of hate. Racism has been an issue for decades and it is still an issue today. It will continue until this world is through. Some racism is learned in the household and it has been a part of our society for decades. So many Blacks left the South to avoid some of the racist attitudes of whites. They were seeking better opportunities that were limited growing up in the deep South because of the attitudes of whites.

I have been examining the attitudes and behaviors of whites for many years. I have had a substantial amount of exposure to them by working with them and attaining friendships with them. We have been trying to comprehend why so many of us have been murdered by cops. The focus is to try to alleviate and prevent cops from killing us upon our encounters with them as murders continue to occur. The last thing that you want to do as an African American is to irritate them and end up being shot and killed when they approach you and stop you on the road. When they do administer excessive force, you are caught off guard. You become hostile and give them control of the situation. Once you become hostile, you place yourself in danger and you might wind up being shot. We should always try to cooperate with them so that you will not be shot for running or create any unnecessary anger from them. Our lives are very important and we should always cooperate with them no matter how mad or pissed we are because we were pulled over and stopped by the cops.

Some Blacks do place themselves in harm's way when they run and don't cooperate with the cops. Once you create an altercation with them, they take control and wind up taking your life when you could have done everything that they told you to do. We should never resist. Resistance can lead to your demise or even death. The cop's anger becomes very dangerous and this can lead to your destruction. One of the reasons that blacks run from the cops is because they might have a warrant, outstanding tickets, child support, or a ticket. If you have these blemishes on your record, it isn't worth being shot or running away from a cop. Life is more important than risking it for violations that you might have accumulated on your police record. Don't be afraid to swallow your pride if it means that your life is going to be spared or saved. Life is a precious gift that should never be taken for granted or compromised for any circumstances. Every situation has to be examined before we can cast judgment on bad cops. Body cams have been some help in determining what happened at the scene of the crime or the encounter that blacks have with the police.

We do need better police reform and this doesn't entail the defunding of the police department. This is one of the dumbest ideas that I have ever heard. We need cops to serve and protect society and we don't want to dismantle and abolish the police department. We do need services that work with cops to help alleviate some of the issues involving encounters with cops. They need to train cops on dealing with all ethnic groups in society especially people of color. Training will focus on dealing with certain populations. Training that would involve and focus on de-escalating certain situations so that they will not lead to the death of a human being. The focus should also concentrate on the importance of valuing human life. We aren't trying to turn cops into wimps but we do want them to feel valued and appreciated when certain situations lead to violence, unrest, riots, and other negative aspects of society. It has to be a give and take that benefits all sectors of society. The last thing that we want to do is discourage people from going into law enforcement.

<u>Comments:</u> Some of us will eventually have an encounter with the cops and some of us might never be stopped by the police. I never labeled cops as an enemy. Some of them don't like blacks but this doesn't make me hate all cops. We do have control of our behavior and this would mean when you are stopped by the police. I never demonstrated any kind of aggression when they

stopped me even when I knew that I didn't do anything wrong or when stopped for a stupid reason that might lead to my death. When I grew up in the '70s, police did seem to demonstrate less anger towards citizens. This is just my personal opinion.

Chapter Eleven

The Law Enforcement (Police) Quiz

Please take this quiz as a method of prevention when you are stopped or pulled over by law enforcement. Below are some of the most obvious reasons why cops stop drivers. There are **25 questions.** Each question is worth 4 points to equal 100 points. Answers will follow.

1. You are driving down the road and then you notice that you were in a 50mph speeding zone and when you looked at the speedometer it was 60mph. The cop's lights start flashing and coming up behind you: **Do You……**

    a. Stop the car immediately when you notice that the cops are behind you
    b. Stop the car and jump out of the car and make a run for it
    c. Ignore the cops and keep driving, thinking that your car is faster than the cops

2. You are talking on your cellphone and the cops catch you and pull you over: **Do you...**

    a. Hide the cellphone and pretend that you weren't using the cellphone
    b. Try to throw the cellphone out of the window before the cops get up to your car
    c. Admit your guilt and cooperate with the cops because you were caught

3. You just left a party, and your driving becomes hazardous, and the cop's car is flashing his lights coming behind you: **Do you....**

    a. Ignore the police and keep going, jeopardizing the safety of others
    b. Pullover immediately and wait for the cops to come up to your vehicle
    c. Curse at the cops when they come to your car and deny doing anything wrong

4. You have some driving violations on your record and you are stopped by the cops for speeding. When the cops come up to your car: **Do you...**

    a. Speed off and try to leave the scene
    b. Pretend that you don't have any outstanding traffic violations

   c. Wait patiently for the cops to come up to your car and tell them about the violations

5. You were caught by the police driving at night with one bad headlight when the cops see you: **Do you...**

   a. Stop immediately when you see the cop's flashers
   b. Keep going and hope that you can escape the cops
   c. Lie to the cops about not knowing about the missing headlight when you did know

6. Cops noticed that you were tailgating and he is coming behind you with his flashers on **Do you...**

   a. Keep going with the anticipation that your car is faster than the cops'
   b. Stop and listen to the cops and see what you are being charged with
   c. Refuse to get out of your car and get hostile with the cops and swing at the cops

7. You have been caught making improper lane changes by the cops: **Do you...**

   a. Speed off when the cops come up to your car
   b. Cause an altercation with the cops because you felt you didn't do anything wrong

c. Admit to the cops that you realized what you were doing wrong and cooperate

8. You were on the road driving below the required speed limit and a cop spots you on the road: **Do you...**

    a. Stop immediately once you see the cop's flashers
    b. Ignore the cop's flashers and keep going, hoping to escape the cops
    c. Pretend that you don't have a clue as to why the cops stopped you

9. The cops spotted you not wearing a seatbelt and a cop's car is approaching you: **Do you....**

    a. Try and put on the seatbelt before the cop comes up to your car
    b. Admit to the cop that you weren't wearing the seatbelt
    c. Refuse to cooperate with the cop on all levels

10. It is late at night around 2:00 A.M. and you have to drive to an area that is highly populated with police looking for speeders: **Do you...**

    a. Just wait until daylight before you take your trip and drive the normal speed limit
    b. Take your chance and drive through a highly-populated area where cops are checking for speeders

c. Forget about the trip and take it when fewer cops are checking for speeders

11. You were caught selling drugs on the street and got caught by cops: **Do you...**

a. Do you struggle with the cops, resist when they try to handcuff you
b. Cooperate with the cops and allow them to handcuff you without anger or aggression
c. Run when you see the cops coming towards you

12. The cops stop you and three other friends in the car for speeding and you know you have drugs in the car: **Do you...**

a. Speed off when the cop comes near the car and throw the drugs out the window
b. Lie to the cops that you didn't know who the drugs belong to
c. Be truthful with the cop and tell him who the drugs belong to

13. You are in the grocery store and you see someone stealing some items out of the store, cops approach you as a witness: **Do you...**

a. Cooperate with the cops and explain that you saw the entire incident

b. Leave the store when you see the cops coming towards you
c. Lie to the cops that you didn't see anything and don't say a word

14. You just happen to be visiting a friend and she noticed that her $300.00 was stolen and you know who took the money. She calls the cops: **Do you...**
    a. Tell your friend that you know who took the money
    b. Do you wait and tell the cops who had stolen the money
    c. Pretend that you do not know who had stolen the money

15. You were on your way home and you ran a red light and some cops spotted you: **Do you...**

    a. Keep speeding as fast as you can so that you will not be stopped by cops
    b. Stop immediately when you see the cop's flashers behind you
    c. Take no responsibility for your actions knowing you could have killed someone

16. You decided to get into your friend's stolen car and the cops have spotted you and they turn on the flashers: **Do you...**

a. Tell your friend that is driving the car not to stop
b. Tell your friend to stop the car so you both can make a run for it
c. Tell your friend to stop the car and wait for the police to come up to the car

17. You knew that your sister was using some stolen credit cards, the cops come to the home for questioning about the incident: **Do you…**

a. Pretend that you aren't aware of the incident and tell your sister to lie
b. Inform the police that you are aware of the entire incident
c. Tell your sister to cooperate with the police and tell the truth

18. You are living in an apartment with your brother, you know that he is writing bad checks to a local grocery store. The cops come to your apartment because they suspect that someone in your apartment is guilty: **Do you…**

a. Tell your brother to stop writing bad checks
b. Join in with your brother and start writing bad checks
c. Cooperate with the cops and explain to them that you know who is writing the bad checks

19. You are working for a Juvenile Detention Center and there is a rumor going around that someone is selling illegal drugs in the facility and you are aware of who is selling the drugs: **Do you...**

    a. Go to your supervisor and inform him that you are aware of who is selling the drugs
    b. Keep your mouth shut because you don't want to hurt any of your coworkers
    c. Tell the coworker to stop selling the drugs so that they will not be caught

20. Your brother is married to a woman who pretends that she isn't married so that she can receive Section 8 housing assistance and you are aware of this: **Do you...**

    a. Keep their secret knowing that your brother and his wife are involved in fraud
    b. Convince your brother to tell his wife to stop indulging in fraudulent behavior
    c. Contact the Department of Social Services and inform them that your sister-in-law is involved in a scam so that your brother will not be arrested for fraud

21. Your mother has been abused by your father for years. He recently beat her up and she called the police to the house and you witnessed the incident: **Do you...**

a. Tell the cops that you didn't witness any such incident
b. Cooperate with the cops and explain to them what you witnessed
c. Convince your mother to be honest with the cops and tell the truth

22. The cops stopped you because they suspect that you are driving around in a car with an unregistered weapon: **Do you...**

a. Run and jump out of the vehicle when the cops approach your vehicle
b. Don't allow the cops to search the vehicle knowing you have the weapon in the car
c. Allow the cops to search the vehicle without any kind of anger or hostility

23. You are stopped by the cops because you are driving with an expired license tab: **Do you...**

a. Speed off when the cops get up to your car
b. Admit to the cops that you were aware of driving with an expired license tab
c. Refuse to cooperate with the cops and ignore all instruction by the cops

24. Your best friend has been selling illegal drugs in your neighborhood for years and the cops have a lead on the

person and you know the identity of the drug seller. The cops start questioning you: **Do you...**

a. Cooperate with the cops and inform them that you know who has been selling the drugs in the neighborhood
b. Go to your friend and warn him that the cops are on his trail
c. Lie to cops that you don't know of anyone selling drugs in the neighborhood

25. You were involved in a hit and run accident and you have been located by someone that turned in your license plate number. The cops come knocking at your door: **Do you...**

    a. Lie to the cops when they start questioning you about the incident
    b. Refuse to cooperate with the cops on any level and become irate with the cops
    c. Admit to the cops that you were the one driving the car that killed a pedestrian
    d. As you see the cops come up to your door, run and sneak out the backdoor

Comments: When you are stopped by the cops, the last thing that you want to do is become hostile with the cops or behave in any kind of aggressive manner. Please make sure that you don't get into a struggle that will cause them to shoot you. Don't run away from cops under any circumstances that might lead them to shoot at you. It is important not to exert any anger from the cops because this might lead to your demise or death. You should remain calm and always follow the instruction that they give you. You should never cause any kind of altercation with them especially when your life might be in danger. Please remember to always do what the cops ask you to do when you are stopped and raise both hands when they tell you to get out of the car to help deescalate the situation as much as possible.

The Key to Success Poem
By William Author Ward

The Key to Success!

Happiness comes not from having much to live on
but having much to live for.
Success never resides in the world of weak wishes,
but in the palace of purposeful plans and
prayerful persistence.

Pessimism achieves no success over persistence.
Temporary defeat never spells total failure;
one victory never assures permanent success.

Real success is one who makes
his mark in life without smearing others.
Excellence without effort is as futile
as progress without preparation
Work can be our friend or foe, or joy or our woe.

Success, like happiness, is more than a destination -
it is a venture; more than an achievement - it is an attitude.
The greatest failure is the failure to try.
Alter your attitude and you will change your life.

Who seeks success, let him prepare.
Improvement is the son of discontent;
success is the offspring of preparation.
To emphasize the positive - the affirmative -
is to travel the high road of joy.

Chapter Twelve

Final Thoughts

This book was a very exciting journey that took me back down memory lane rehashing the past to the present. It covers my trajectory growing up as a child and as a teenager in Gary. This book was started at the height of the COVID-19 Pandemic that has affected the entire universe in a very tragic manner. It surged all around the world. Cases surged in the Midwestern States around 2019 to 2021. The pandemic has been catastrophic for many cities and towns in the United States. It has forced people into poverty. Unemployment became a serious disease. People lost their businesses because of lockdowns with the spread of the virus. The impact that this virus has had on the economy was devastating. The virus continues to affect the United States and other countries.

Unrest continues in the United States because of the killing of Blacks in certain cities. This has led to peaceful protests, riots, looting, and other ethical and unethical issues. Chaos, discomfort, and uncertainty have become a problem in the United States. It has been very disturbing to me as a human being to see so much distress, pain, and agony in the world because of the brutality by police officers. Some blacks have been killed without dignity without any value of human life. We all are entitled to the American Dream but it hasn't existed for some Blacks for decades when this is compared to the plight of White America.

I am so glad that I took advantage of the opportunities that were available to me in the late seventies by finishing high school and going to college. This was my ticket out of some of the despair that I experienced growing up in an all-black community. We did have some challenges when my mother was on ADC (Aid for Dependent Children). Society wasn't going to place me in any category and tell my story. I am very proud of my accomplishments that guided me to a very happy retirement. Many negative things came knocking at my door. They weren't going to derail me from reaching my ultimate goal in life and that was to be very successful. My perseverance, tenacity, ambition, and determination led me to a very Happy Ending and I have realized that Dreams Do Come True. I am a great example.

This is one of the reasons that I wanted to share this book with you. There are many happy endings in all ethnic groups and people of color. Some of my other family members have success stories and some of them didn't as I indicated in a previous chapter of this book. Some of my brothers succeeded in college and went on to live very happy and productive lives in the same manner as I did. Other relatives have also attended college with much success. These people have made very good choices and decisions during their journey in life. You have to crawl before you walk. All these people are good but some of them ventured down the wrong road and bad choices have been their Achilles heel.

As African Americans, there is still hope when we can learn from the mistakes of the past and search for a brighter future. We have a right to look into the future considering all the roadblocks and some of the obstacles that have crossed our paths during our life's journey. There are more opportunities today than ever before as compared to the early seventies and eighties. Nothing comes to a dreamer but success. We have to be willing to pursue our dreams and not allow society to continue to perpetuate the stereotypes of our people. Our journey will continue to be a challenge and this journey doesn't have to be flawed by skeletons that have haunted us for years. We have been mistreated and treated badly by law enforcement. It does seem as if we have been plagued with destruction because so many black men have been killed by the police. Confidence is something that we will continue to strive for even when things have happened to us that have been too hard to bear. This book was written and created for the world to read especially African Americans to demonstrate that our future becomes brighter each day that we are on this earth. This book will also help other ethnic groups to understand who we are and understand some of the struggles that we have had in the past and present. I wanted to write this book in an attempt to demonstrate that we have learned from the past and not to continue to make the same mistakes that have somewhat led to our demise as human beings. We cannot keep repeating the ills of the past, this would include breaking the law, stealing, selling drugs, killing each other over drugs, rioting, looting, and other unlawful activities that have destroyed African Americans for decades. The focus should be on decreasing the incarceration of black men. This is a very important priority. Black violence needs to stop in our neighborhoods and cities around the world. We need to value the life of all human beings and especially our people. You don't have Asians, and other groups killing each other over drugs, etc. We can learn things from other ethnic groups that are positive.

We are seeing some of the incarceration rates decrease and I hope that this continues.

Some things are becoming positive in the life of African Americans. I think that more of us are going to college and developing our businesses. We are taking advantage of some of the incentives that other ethnic groups are receiving. We need to focus on not becoming victims in a society where the world has been unkind and cruel in some aspects of our journey in history. Blacks have made some remarkable strides and achievements during the Civil Rights Era and we are continuing to move forward positively. The future can be very productive with the right attitude. Attitude is a major component in moving forward in life. It gives you the energy to excel with ambition in life. The blame game is old news as we move forward in this life. We have to remove all the thorns in our backs if we want to succeed in life. So many of us have achieved that goal but there is more work to be done. Achievement comes in all colors and ethnic groups. Blacks want a piece of that pie because we are entitled to reap the rewards just like other ethnic groups in the world. We shouldn't be deterred by how we are portrayed in this world by some people because of some of the violence that people have seen on television. We have many success stories and will continue to share them with the world. WE have so many things to offer this world and we must believe that.

One thing that I want to stress is that we need to think about investing money in the right things excluding things that don't grow in value such as hair weaves, Air Jordan shoes, etc. The value of these things dissipates very rapidly. We need to invest in things that are going to bring us more equity in life. Invest in education, stocks, annuities, and other things that will make us money. We have to live beyond today and lay out a strong foundation for the future that will keep us financially stable in the next decade and beyond the next decades.

I honestly and wholeheartedly hope that you have enjoyed reading this book just as much as I have enjoyed writing it. We all should be excited about what is coming in the future. We do want to make sure that we always have some plans for tomorrow. Life is dance and it is the ambition that takes the lead. We all are tired of turning on the television and hearing that some black man was killed by the police or hearing about the violence in cities with a higher black population. Black-on-black crime has to stop and only we can change this course. When we are included in the news, we want it to be portrayed as positive images that reflect our ambition and talents in this world. We need to hear more success stories about African Americans that include ordinary people instead of always hearing about athletes, actors, singers, etc. Common people are just as important. We need to eradicate the false hopes of becoming professional athletes, movie stars, rap artists, and careers that involve very little educational training. A college degree isn't for everyone but it might take you places where you wouldn't be able to go as an uneducated person. You can lose a job and other things but a college degree is something that you will have until you die and it can't be taken away.

There are scientists, entrepreneurs, doctors, teachers, and other professionals that have made such an impressive impact on America when it comes to African Americans. It is terrible how we are portrayed and projected on television with the housewives' series. You would think that all black women do is fight and are in conflict with each other all the time. The altercations are embarrassing for our dignity and the majority of black women don't conduct themselves in that kind of fashion, fighting, cursing, pulling hair, etc. People don't hang around in the same circle of people where there is so much conflict. Your reputation is more important than being on some low-rated television shows. Integrity is more important than the amount of money that you might make. It isn't worth destroying your reputation as an African American. We are so much better than that. When shows become violent, they have lost their value in society.

Comments: I am not going to write Gary off because there is hope when things seem too hard to bear. Some of these black communities are challenged because they have been neglected and abandoned for years which influenced their demise. There needs to be more investments in deprived areas with a vision that can re-create these communities and move forward positively. When finances are depleted from an area, crime rises to astronomical numbers. I am going to be very optimistic about the future as we continued to deal with issues that have destroyed communities of color. There is such a thing as rebirth and it can be achieved through perseverance, determination, creativity, hope, investment, and other creative techniques to revive hurting black communities in the United States.

As we move beyond 2021, we have to remember that we have seen deprived and neglected communities rise from the ashes and become vibrant again in some of the worst areas in the United States. We all strive to live in safe communities that provide opportunities for all races of people. Black Communities need to have access to resources that are so readily available in rich suburban areas in the United States. We have known from past experiences that high unemployment areas lead to high crime, drug use, poverty, systemic racism, systemic poverty, and other evils of society that have plagued black communities over the years. As we move forward, there is always hope when we think that situations are so severe and out of our reach.

The Resource Library

Here are some books that might serve as resources that address some of the major issues in our black communities etc. These books are available at your local library or they can be purchased at a bookseller in your community.

Afrika, Llaila O. *Controlling Understanding, and Raising Black Children: Infants to Teenagers*. 2017. 516 pages.
A comprehensive holistic guide for techniques and skills for disciplining and controlling children and teens. Proper growth and development schedule of black children. Emotional and behavioral problem remedies. Learn the early signs and symptoms of children's behavioral and emotional problems.

Bivins, Kenn. *39 Lessons for Black Boys and Girls*. 2020. 1-4. 432p. *The 39 Lessons Series*.
The 39 Lessons Series is a compilation of all four *39 Lessons* books intended to promote self-esteem, wisdom, and excellent decision-making for children. This best-selling collection is a staple for every home, classroom, and library where children and young people learn and play.

Black, Ian Michael. *A Better Man: A (Mostly Serious) Letter to My Son*. 2020. 304 pages.
A poignant look at boyhood, in the form of a heartfelt letter from comedian Michael Ian Black to his teenage son before he leaves for college, and a radical plea for rethinking masculinity and teaching young men to give and receive love.

Brown, Trin A Green. *Parenting for Liberation: A Guide for Raising Black Children*. 2020. 220 pages.
This book speaks directly to parents raising Black children in a world of racialized violence, this guidebook combines powerful storytelling with practical exercises, encouraging readers to imagine methods of parenting routed in liberation rather than fear.

Effective Black Parenting: The Proven Program to Help in Raising Proud, Confident and Healthy African American Children (Parent's Handbook). 1996. 152 pages.
This book explains the most important components of raising proud, confident, and healthy African American Children. A go-to guide with great ideas for parenting and assisting children with becoming productive and successful human beings in a very challenging society that has been difficult for some African Americans.

Holmes, Jasmine L. *Mother to Son: Letters to a Black Boy on Identity and Hope*. 2020. 160 pages.
This book addresses letters to a boy who is loved by his parents. Inquisitive, fiercely affectionate, staunchly opinionated, he sees

the world through eyes of wonder and has yet to become jaded by society's cruelty. He will grow up with stories of having been made to feel 'other' because of the color of his skin.

Kunjufu, Dr. Jawanza. *Counting the Conspiracy to Destroy Black Boys*, Vols. 1-3. 2020. 38 pages.
This book gives excellent advice to parents, educators, community, and church members ensuring that African American boys grow up to be strong, committed, and responsible African American men. This book does answer such questions as to why are there more black boys in remedial and special education classes than girls? When do African American boys see positive black male role models and other questions pertinent to Black Boys?

Kunjufu, Dr. Jawanza. *Developing Positive Self-Images and Discipline in Black Children*. 1984. 116 pages.
The relationship between self-esteem and student achievement is analyzed in this book. When a child develops a sense of worth and high self-esteem, this lays down the foundation for success and other self-motivating principles. This kind of behavior should be encouraged by parents.

Mendoza, Muffy. *The Brown Mama Mindset: A Blueprint for Black Moms on Life, Love and Home*. 2018. 276.
This is a practical guide to learning to love yourself. It is a black parenting book, relationship book, and self-care guide all-in-one; broken into short, power-packed chapters and activities.

Plus, it is one of the few parenting books written for black moms, by a black mom.

Muhammad, Mr. Lawrence. *Parenting Secrets of Black Millionaires: 6 True Stories Showing How to Unlock the Generational Wealth-Building Power Within Your Children.* Volumes 1- 2. 2020. 258 pages.
This book explains how so many parents have a desire to give their children a better life, but they don't know how to get started, so they avoid having the money conversations altogether. This book talks about exact methods that millionaires' parents used to rear their children to success. It will also help you identify poor financial habits that you may be unknowingly passed on to your children.

Patton, Stacey. *Spare the Kids: Why Whipping Children Won't Save Black America*. 2017. 248 pages.
This book demonstrates effective methods to teach respect and protect black children from the streets, incarceration encounters with racism, or worse. Dr. Stacey Patton's research suggests that corporal punishment is a crucial factor explaining why black folks are subject to disproportionately higher rates of school suspensions and expulsions, criminal prosecutions, improper mental health diagnosis, child abuse cases, and foster care placements, which too often funnel abused and traumatized children into the prison system.

Wealth, Anne-Lyse. *Dream of Legacy: Raising Strong and Financially Secure Black Kids*. 2020. 155 pages.

The time has never been auspicious for Black people to control their finances and achieve financial freedom. You need to have economic leverage which is the key priority in the fight for equality and justice. The author shares financial knowledge to help build generational wealth in the Black community and close the racial wealth gap.

Crime

Gilliard, Dominique DuBois. *Advocating for Justice That Restores*. 2018. 240 pages.
The United States has more people locked up in jails, prisons, and detention centers than any other country in the history of the world. Blacks have the highest incarceration in the United States. Mass incarceration has become a lucrative industry and the criminal justice system is plagued with bias and unjust practices. Dominique Gilliard explores the history and foundation of mass incarceration examining Christianity's role in its evolution and expansion. The church has the power to help transform our criminal justice system that will benefit all ethnic groups especially Blacks.

Harper, Hill. *Letters to an Incarcerated Brother: Encouragement, Hope, and Healing for Inmates and Their Loved Ones*. 2014. 400 pages.
This book acknowledges the disturbing statistics on African-American incarcerations. Harper addresses the specific needs of inmates. He has a powerful message from the heart that provides

advice and inspiration in the face of despair along with encouraging words for restoring a sense of self-worth. This book is uplifting and insightful and provides the hope and inspiration inmates and their families need.

Jackson, Adrian O. *Encounters with Police: A Black Man's Guide to Survival.* 1st Edition. 2015. 106 pages.
This book provides advice to African American boys and men on how to survive encounters with police. It also provides ideas on how to think about interaction with police to lower chances of escalation. It also provides practical step-by-step guidelines on how to respond to police when pulled over for traffic stops and when stopped for questioning outside of traffic encounters.

Zack, Naomi. *White Privilege and Black Rights: The Injustice of U.S. Police Racial Profiling and Homicide.* 2015. 154 pages.
This book examines racial profiling in American policing, Naomi Zack argues against white privilege discourse while introducing a new theory of applicative justice. Zack draws a line between rights and privileges and between justice and existing laws to make sense of the current crisis.

Education

Davis, Sampson. *We Beat the Streets: How a Friendship Pact Led to Success.* 2006. 194 pages.
A book that examines the lives of three men who grew up in the streets of Newark, New Jersey explaining how they avoided

the evils of drug dealing, gangs, and prison to become doctors in the medical and dental profession. They took advantage of the opportunities that were available to them with a lot of determination and perseverance. They supported each other on the road to success.

Garrett, Kent. *The Last Negroes At Harvard: The Class of 1963 and the 18 Men Who Changed Harvard Forever.* 2020. 32 pages.
The untold story of the Harvard Class of 1963, whose Black students fought to create their own identities on the cusp between integration and affirmative action. This is a remarkable story of brilliant, singular boys whose identities were changed at and by Harvard, and who, in turn, changed Harvard.

Goggins, David. *Can't Hurt Me: Master Your Mind and Defy the Odds.* 2018. 364 pages.
This book explains how a depressed, overweight young man with no future joined the Armed Forces with complete training, to become a Navy Seal, Army Ranger, and Air Force Tactical Air Controller to set numerous records in endurance events inspiring other African American men and boys.

Harper, Hill. *Letters to a Young Brother: Manifest Your Destiny.* 2007. 176 pages.
An inspiring book with a compilation of letters that provide wisdom, guidance, and heartfelt insight to assist African American men with their path to success. The letters address the tough issues that face young black people today especially young black men.

Howard, Tyrone C. *Black Male(d): Peril and Promise in the Education of African American Males (Multicultural Education)*. 51 Books. 2013. 208 pages.
A good that examines the chronic underperformance of African American males in U.S. schools around the country. City a plethora of disturbing academic outcomes for Black males. The book focuses on the historical, structural, educational, psychological, emotional, and cultural factors that influence the teaching and learning process of black students.

McRaven, Admiral William H. *Make Your Bed: Little Things That Can Change Your Life*. 2017. 144 pages.
This book was written by the former U.S. Navy General who discusses how life and powerful life lessons can change anyone. He explains how determination, compassion, honor, and courage can affect your destiny in life. It provides simple wisdom, practical advice, and words of encouragement that will inspire readers to achieve more, even in life's darkest moments.

Patterson, James T. *Brown vs. Board of Education: A Civil Rights Milestone and Its Troubled Legacy*. 2002. 320 pages.
A book about a historical ruling that struck down state-sponsored racial segregation in America's public schools. A landmark that changed the dynamics in the education system for decades. Patterson examines some questions that still surface about the case. This case is fifty years old and we still explore the contents of this document.

The Black Family

Anderson, Maggie. *Our Black Year: One Family's Quest to Buy Black in America's Racially Divided Economy.* 2013. 320 pages.
A book that focuses on black wealth and the impact that it has on black communities. Some blacks live in economically starved neighborhoods. Black wealth is about one-tenth of white wealth and black businesses of all other racial groups in every measure of success. One problem is that black consumers—unlike consumers of other ethnicities choose not to support black-owned businesses.

Connor, Michael E. *Black Fathers: An Invisible Presence in America,* Second Edition. 2011. 302 pages.
This book offers a broader, more positive picture of African American fathers. Featuring case studies of African-descended fathers, this book brings to life the challenges of being a black father in America. It also covers the impact of health issues on Black fathers and their children. The need for therapeutic interventions to aid in the healing of fathers and their children.

Fievre, M.J. *Raising Confident Black Kids: A Comprehensive Guide for Empowering Parents and Teachers of Black Children.* 2021. 254 pages.
Discusses everything Black and multi-racial families need to know to raise empowered, confident children. From the realities of living while Black to age-appropriate ways to discuss racism with your children. This is a much-needed resource for parents of Black kids in the United States.

Franklin, Nancy Boyd. *Black Families in Therapy: Understanding the African American Experience*. 2006. 368.
A book to help professionals and students understand and address cultural and racial issues in therapy. It focuses and explores the problems facing African American communities at different socioeconomic levels, expands major therapeutic concepts and models to be more relevant to the experiences of African American families and individuals.

Hill, Robert B. *The Strengths of Black Families*. 2003. 112 pages
This book was written to provide a rare perspective focusing on the assets and resilience of black families. This book has stimulated numerous studies of the strengths of African American, Hispanic American, Asian American, and Native American families.

McAdoo, Harriette Pipes. *Black Families*. 2006. 384 pages.
A book on the positive dimensions of African American families. An assessment of things to help blacks live and exist in an environment that has been hostile at times. Cross-disciplinary in nature, the book boasts contributions from such fields as family studies, anthropology, education, psychology, social work, and public policy.

Protest, Rioting and Looting

Charles River Editors. *The New York City Blackout of 1977: The History of the Power Failure That Led to Looting and Arson Across the Big Apple*. 2016. 58 pages.

This book describes how looting and arson had such a negative impact on the Big Apple (New York). The Blackout of 1977 caused crime that permeated throughout the city. Blacks engaged themselves in heavy looting and arson that was devastating to the city and businesses in the area.

Gillion, Daniel Q. *The Loud Minority: Why Protest Matter in American Democracy,* Book 20. 2020. 219 pages.
The Loud Minority describes this view by demonstrating that voters are directly informed and influenced by protest activism. It talks about the supposed wedge that exists between protestors in the streets and the voters at home. When protests grow in America, every aspect of the electoral process is influenced by this loud minority, benefiting the political party perceived to be the most supportive of the messaging from the protestors.

Kluger, Jeffrey. *Raise Your Voice: 12 Protests That Shaped America.* 2020. 224 pages.
We have experienced protests and demonstrations as they spread throughout the United States at the height of the BLMM in recent years. They have pushed for change on many issues, including women's rights, racial equality, climate change, gun control, LGBTQ rights, and more. These marches may seem like a new trend, they are the continuation of a long line of Americans taking their feet and raising their voices to cry out for justice.

Black Homicide in America

Aspholm, Roberto R. *Views from the Streets: The Transformation of Gang and Violence on Chicago's South Side (Studies in Transgression)*. 2020. 288 pages.
A look at the violence in Chicago. The city's staggering levels of violence and entrenched gang culture occupy a central place in the national discourse, yet remain poorly understood and are often stereotyped. The book explains the dramatic transformation of black street gangs on Chicago's South Side during the 21st Century, shedding new light on why gang violence persists and what might be done to address it.

Cooney, Mark. *Is Killing Wrong?: A Study in Pure Sociology (Studies in Pure Sociology)*. 2012. 272 pages.
This book provides the most comprehensive assessment of homicide of pure sociology. It draws on data from well over 100 societies, including the modern-day United States. It examines conduct and how society is affected by this kind of behavior. It explains how this conduct is wrong.

Landrum, Maurice L. *Gangsters, Narcotics, Homicide: "Protecting the Thin Blue Line."* 2020. 248 pages.
A gook that looks at the law enforcement career of Maurice L. Landrum from childhood to being sworn in as a Lost Angeles Police Officer. It is a true story about street life in Los Angeles and career survival within the Los Angeles Police Department. It targets the struggles to maintain peace and calm where vio-

lence, narcotics, and homicides significantly affect Los Angeles and other cities in the United States.

Simon, David. *Homicide: A Year on the Killing Streets*. 2006. 672 pages.
A visit to Baltimore, Maryland wherein every three days another citizen is shot, stabbed, or bludgeoned to death on the streets. It tells the true story of a year on the violent streets of an American city. This narrative follows Donald Worden, a veteran investigator, Harry Edgerton, a black detective in a mostly white unit; Tom Pellegrin, an earnest rookie who takes on the year's most difficult case.

Zack, Naomi. *White Privilege and Black Rights: The Injustice of U.S. Police Racial Profiling and Homicide.* 2015. 154 pages.
Examining racial profiling in American policing, Naomi argues against white privilege discourse while introducing a new theory of applicable justice. Zack draws clear lines between rights and privileges and between justice and existing laws to make sense of the current crisis. This urgent and immediate analysis of the killings of unarmed black men by police officers shows how racial profiling matches statistics of the prison population with no regard to the constitutional rights of the many innocent people of color.

References Cited

Beer, Todd. "Police Killing Blacks. Do Black Lives Matter?" The Society Pages. May 26, 2020. https://www.thesocietypages.org/toolbox/police-the-killing-of-blacks/

Bond, M. Jermane, Ph.D. "Lagging Life Expectancy for Black Men: A Health Imperative." *American Journal of Public Health*. 2016 of July. Pages 1167 – 1169. https://ncbi.nih.gov/pmc/articles/PMC-4984780

Bridges, Brian, Ph.D. "African Americans and College Education by Numbers." 2020. UNCF. https://uncf.org/the-lastest/african-and-college-education-by-the-number?

Carter, Kellie. "The Double Standard of the American Riot." *The Atlantic*. Culture. June 1, 2020. https://theatlantic.com/culture/archive/2020/06/riots-are-american-way-george-floyd-protests/612466

City Lab. "What We Forgot About the 1992 L.A. Riots." https://www.citylab.com/equity/2017/04/what-was-lost-in-the-fires-of-the-la-riots

Gramlich. John. "The Gap Between the Number of Blacks and Whites in Prison Is Shrinking." *Fact Tank: News in the Numbers*. April 30, 2020. https://pewresearch.org/fact-tank/2019/04/30/shrinking-gap-between-number-of-blacks-and-whites-in-prison/

Golden, Sherita Hill. "COVID-19 Vaccines and People of Color." Health. John Hopkins Medicine. 2021. https://hopkinsmedicine.org/health/conditions-and-diseases/coronavirus/covid19-vaccines-and-people-of-color

Hagler, Jamal. "6 Things You Should Know About Women of Color and the Criminal Justice System." Center for American Progress. March 16, 2016. https://americanprogress.org/issues/criminal-justice/news/2016/03/16/133438/6-things-you-should-know-about-women-of-color-and-the-criminal-justice-system/

Hay, Mark. "Marijuana's Early History in the United States." March 31, 2015. https://vice.com/en_us/article/xd7d8d/how-marijuana-came-the-united-states-456
History.com Editors. "Cocaine." July 14, 2020. https://www.history.com/topics/crime/history-of-cocaine

History.com Editors. "Marijuana." May 31, 2017. https://www.history.com/topics/crime/history-of-marijuana

Hudgins, John. "Black Homicide." *The Baltimore Sun*. April 03, 2020. https://www.baltimoresun.com/opinion/op-ed/bs-ed-op-o406-black-crime-20200403-lyiri4nzuxks6i2h6mhirtq-story.html.

Humphreys, Keith. "There's Been a Big Decline in Black Incarceration Rate. Economic Policy." February 10, 2016. https://washingtonpost.com/news/wonk/wp/2016/02/10/almost-nobody-is-paying-attention-to-this-massive-change-in-criminal-justice/

Hutchinson, Bill. "Police Declare Riots as Protests Turn Violent in Cities." *ABC News*. July 26, 2020. https://abcnews.go.com/us/police-declare-riots-protests-turn-violent-cities-nationwide/story?id=7199483

Hymowitz, Kay S. "The Black Family: 40 Years of Lies." Politics and Law. Summer 2005. The Social Order; Public Safety. *City Journal*. https://www.city.journal.org/html/black-family-40-years-lies-12872.html

Khazan, Olga. "Why People Loot." Health. *The Atlantic*. June 2, 2020. https://www.theatlantic.com/health/archive/2020/06/why-people-loot/612577/

Libassi, CJ. "The Neglected College Race Gap: Racial Disparities Among College Completers." Center for American Progress. May 23, 2018.

https://americanprogress.org/issues/eduction-postsecondary/reports/2018/05/23/451186/neglected-college-race-racial-gap

Loveless, Becton. “Benefits of Earning a College Degree.” Education Center 2020. https://www.educationcorner.com/benefit-of-earning-a-college-degree-html.

Lee, Lethia. “Nutrition and the African-American Diet.” *The Sampson Independent*. November 14, 2020. https://www.clintonnc.com/features/lifestyle/27515/nutrition-and-the-african-american-diet.

Map of Indiana. 2020. Nations Online. https://www.nationsonline.org/oneworld/map/usa/wisconsin-map.html.
Marshall, William F. “Coronavirus Infection by Race: What’s Behind the Health Disparities.” The Mayo Clinic. August 13, 2020. https://www.mayoclinic.org/diseases-conditions/coronavirus/expert-answers/coronavirus- infection-by-race/faq-20488802

Maxwell, Connor and Solomon, Danyelle. “Mass Incarceration, Stress, and Black Infant Mortality: A Case Study in Structural Racism.” The Center for American Progress. June 5, 2018. https://americanprogress.org/issues/race/reports/2018/05/451647/mass-incarceration-stress-black-infant-mortality/

McIntosh, Emily. Brooks. “Examining the Black-White Wealth Gap.” Thursday, February 27, 2020.

https://www.brookings.edu/blog/up-front/2020/02/27/examining-the-black-white-wealth-gap.

Moss, Emily. "Examining the Black-White-Wealth Gap." Thursday, February 27, 2020. https://www.brooking.edu/blog/up-front/2020/02/27/examing-the-black-white-wealth-gap/

The National Bureau of Economic Research. "How the 1960's Riots Hurt African Americans." Wednesday, June 3, 2020. https://www.nber.org/digest/sep04/w10243.html

Nellis, Ashley, Ph.D. "The Color of Justice: Racial and Ethnic Disparity in State Prisons." June 14, 2016. https://sentencingproject.org/publications/color-of-justice-racial-and-ethnic-disparity-in-state-prisons/

Newkirk II, Vann. R. "Voter Suppression Is Warping Democracy." *The Atlantic*. July 17, 2018. https://theatlantic.com/politics/archive/2018/07/poll-prri-voter-suppression/565355/

Nolan, Hamilton. "Poverty and Racism Aren't the Same, but Black People Are Getting Screwed by Both." 01/25/16 01:40 PM Filed to Inequality. https://www.gawker.com/poverty-and-racism-aren't-the-same-but-black-people-are-1754950415

NPR. "American Life Expectancy Dropped a Full Year in 1st

Half of 2020." February 18, 2021. https://npr.org/2021/02/18/968791431/american-life-expectancy-dropped-by-a-full-year-in-the-first-half-of-2020.

"Open Wide Our Hearts: The Enduring Call of Love." A Pastoral Letter Against Racism. https://www.Usccb.org/issues-and-action/human-life-and-action/human-life-and-dignity/racism/upload/racism-and-systemic-racism.pdf.

"Popular and Pervasive Stereotypes of African Americans." Smithsonian. National Museum of African American History and Culture. https://nmaahc.si.edu/blog-post/popular-and-pervasive-stereotypes-african-americans

"Race Riots/Teaching Tolerance." https://www.tolerance.org/classroom-resources/texts/race-riots

Report. "College Access Remains Inequitable At Selective Publics." *Inside Higher Ed*. July 21, 2020. https://www.insidehighered.com/news/2020/07/21/inequity-college-access-continues-black- latinx-students-report-finds

"Riots." Iowa Department of Human Rights. https://www.humanrights.iowa.gov/cas/saa/african-american-culture-history/riots.

Schiller, Andrew, Dr. "The Most Dangerous US Neighborhoods of 2018." Crime. November 21, 2018. Neighborhood

Scout. https://www.neighborhoodscout.com/blog/25-most-dangerous-neighborhoods

Semuels, Alana. “States with Large Black Populations Are Stingier with Government Benefits.” Next Economy. June 6, 2017. https://www.theatlantic.com/business/archivel/2017/06/race-safety-net-Welfare/529203

Taylor, Evi. “The Historical Perspectives of Stereotypes on African-American Males.” Springer Link. May 7, 2019. https://link.springer.com/article/10.1007/s41134-019-00096-y.

The Center for Public Integrity. “Analysis: New and Age-Old Voter Suppression Tactics at the Heart of the 2020 Power Struggle.” Barriers to the Ballot Box. October 28, 2020. https://publicintegrity.org/politics/elections/ballotboxbarrier/analysis-voter-suppression-never-went-away-tactics-changed/

Thomas, Anita, Ph.D. APA. “Promoting Culturally Affirming Parenting in African American Parents: Positive Parenting in African American Families.” *CYF News*, April 2017. https:// Apa.org/pi/families/resources/newsletter/2017/04/African-american-parents.

“Welfare Expands in the 1960s: Migration of African Americans from the Rural South, and Its Effects.” Soc 315-Social Welfare. https://www.people.eou.edu/socwel/readings/week-2/welfare-expands-in-the-1960s/

Police Quiz Answers

4 points for each Correct Response

Grading Scale Percentile

A+	97 – 100	Percentile
A	93 – 96	Points
A-	90 – 92	Points
B+	87 – 89	Points
B	83 – 86	Points
B-	80 – 82	Points
C+	77 – 79	Points
C	73 – 76	Points
C-	70 – 72	Points
D+	67 – 69	Points
D	63 – 66	Points
D-	60 – 62	Points
F	Below 60	

Answers to Questions

1. A
2. C

3. B
4. C
5. A
6. B
7. C
8. A
9. B
10. A & C
11. B
12. C
13. A
14. B
15. B
16. C
17. B & C
18. A & C
19. A
20. B & C
21. B & C
22. C
23. B
24. A
25. C

Glossary of Terms

Aid to Families with Dependent Children: was a federal assistance program in effect from 1935 to 1997 created by the Social Security Act and administered by the United States Department of Health and Human Services that provided financial assistance to children whose families had low or no income.

Andrew Michael Manis: Is a historian, author, professor at Middle Georgia State University in Macon, Georgia.

Center for American Progress: is a public policy research and advocacy organization which presents a liberal viewpoint on social and economic issues. It has its headquarters in Washington, D.C.

Centers for Disease Control and Prevention (CDC): Is a national public health institute in the United States. It is a United States federal agency, under the Department of Health and Human Services, and is headquartered in Atlanta, Georgia.

Coronavirus: are a group of RNA viruses that cause diseases in mammals and birds. In humans and birds, they cause respiratory tract infections that can range from mild to lethal. Mild illnesses in humans include some cases of the common cold, while more lethal varieties can cause SARS, MERS, and COVID-19. This virus surged around the world in 2019 – 2021 affecting millions of people.

Crack cocaine: also known simply as crack or rock, is a free base form of cocaine that can be smoked. Crack offers a short, intense high to smokers.

Gary: is a city in Lake County, Indiana, United States, twenty-five miles from downtown Chicago, Illinois. Gary is adjacent to the Indiana Dunes National Park and borders southern Lake Michigan. Gary was named after lawyer Elbert Henry Gary, who was the founding chairman of the United States Steel Corporation.

Incarceration: The act of putting or keeping someone in prison or a place used as a prison for criminal offenders. These offenders have been sentenced and convicted in a court of law for misconduct.

Jim Crow Laws: were state and local laws that enforced racial segregation in the Southern States. These laws were created in the late 19th and early 20th centuries by white Southern Democrat-dominated state legislatures to disenfranchise and remove political and economic gains made by black people during the Reconstruction Period.

Johnson and Johnson Vaccine: a vaccine developed and created to prevent people from catching the COVID-19 Virus and to prevent the virus from spreading.

Law Enforcement (Police): This is the activity of some members of government who act in an organized manner to enforce the law by discovering, deterring, rehabilitating, or punishing people who violate the rules and norms governing that society.

Looting: refers to the act of stealing, or the taking of goods by force, amid a military, political, riots, other social crisis, such as war, natural disasters, rioting.

Mammy: Also spelled Mammie, is a U.S. stereotype, especially in the South, for a black woman who worked in a white family and nursed the family's children. The mammy figure is rooted in the history of slavery in the United States. Black slave women were tasked with domestic and childcare work in white American slaveholding households.

Moderna Vaccine: vaccine developed to stop the spreading of the Coronavirus authorized by the FDA and recommended by the CDC for use in the U.S. for a limited population.

Marijuana: Cannabis, also known as marijuana among other names, is a psychoactive drug from the Cannabis plant used primarily for medical or recreational purposes. The main psychoactive component of cannabis is tetrahydrocannabinol, which is one of 483 known compounds in the plant, including at least sixty-five other cannabinoids, including cannabidiol.

National Center for Health Statistics (NCHS): Is a principal agency of the United States Federal Statistical System, which provides statistical information to guide actions and policies to improve the public health of the American people.

Parenting: or child rearing is the process of promoting and supporting the physical, emotional, social, and intellectual development of a child from infancy to adulthood. Parenting refers to the intricacies of raising a child and not exclusively for a biological relationship.

Pfizer Vaccine: a vaccine developed for the COVID-19 virus authorized by the FDA and recommended by the CDC to use in the United States for a limited population.

Poverty: Poverty is the state of not having enough material possessions or income for a person's basic needs. Poverty includes social, economic, and political elements. Poverty has harmed black populations and other ethnic groups.

Protest: is a public expression of objection, disapproval, or dissent towards an idea or action, typically a political one. Protests can take many different forms, from individual statements to mass demonstrations.

Public Religion Research Institute (PRRI): The Public Religion Research Institute is an American nonprofit, nonpartisan research and education organization that conducts public opinion polls on a variety of different topics, specializing in the quantitative and qualitative study of political issues as they relate to religious values.

Reconstruction Era: the period in history that lasted from 1865 to 1877 following the American Civil War which marked a significant chapter in the history of Civil Rights in the United States.

Riots: a riot is a form of civil disorder commonly characterized by a group lashing out in a violent public disturbance against authority, property, or people.

Systemic Poverty: Systemic poverty refers to the economic exploitation of people who are poor through laws, policies, practices, and systems that perpetuate their impoverished status. Poverty is complex and overlaps with many other social ills and oppressive structures in our society.

Systemic Racism: Institutional racism, also known as systemic racism, is a form of racism that is embedded as a normal practice within society or an organization. It can lead to such issues as discrimination in criminal practice, employment, housing, healthcare, political power, and education, among other issues.

Soul Food: is an ethnic cuisine traditionally prepared and eaten by African Americans, originating in the Southern United States. The cuisine originated with the foods that were given to enslaved West Africans on southern plantations during the American colonial period; however, it was strongly influenced by the traditional practices of West Africans and Native Americans from its inception.

Voter Suppression: is a strategy used to influence the outcome of an election by discouraging and preventing specific groups of people from voting. This was a tactic used to stop Blacks from voting during the Jim Crow Era and beyond which is still an issue today when comes to honoring the right to vote under the Constitution.

Voting Rights Act of 1965: is a landmark piece of federal legislation in the United States designed to eradicate racial discrimination in voting. This legislation was the vehicle that made it possible for Blacks to exercise the right to vote under the 14th and 15th Amendments of the Constitution, especially in the South.

Watermelon: is a flowering plant species of the Cucurbitaceae family. A scrambling and vine-like plant, it was originally domesticated in Africa. It is a highly cultivated fruit worldwide, with more than 100 varieties.

Welfare: is a type of government support intended to ensure that members of a society can meet basic human needs such as food and shelter. President Lyndon B. Johnson passed welfare legislation to assist families that were in need. Blacks that were victims of systemic poverty were available for this kind of assistance and single mothers.

Index

Black Achievement Gap, 75
Black Family, The, 145
Black Homicide, 39
Black Incarceration, 52
Black Stereotypes, 195
Closing the Achievement Gap, 75
Coronavirus, The, 203
COVID-19 Vaccine, 207
Crack Cocaine, 24
Education Disparities, 87
Glossary of Terms, 265
Incarceration of Black Women, 62
Index, 271
Law Enforcement (Police), 211
Law Enforcement Quiz (Police), 219
Law Enforcement Quiz Answers (Police), 263
Life Expectancy of Blacks, 177
Looting, 58
Marijuana, 20
Marijuana – The Effects, 21
Nutrition and Diet of Blacks, 169
Parenting, 157

Perspective, 1
Police and Blacks, 47
Protests and Demonstrations, 56
Race Riots, 44
References Cited, 255
Resource Library, 241
Stories of Bad Behavior, 95
Systemic Poverty, 28
Systemic Racism, 26
Teacher Training, 85
Voter Suppression, 187
Wealth Inequality, 33
Welfare, 28

About the Author

This book is DeVere's debut in the literary world. He has created his very first manuscript (75,000 words) which has taken two years to create. DeVere developed a passion for reading in elementary school according to his elementary school teacher, Ms. Thenora Beard who is ninety years old to this very day. She said that she recalls that DeVere would always challenge the school librarian to buy more books for his grade school library. He enjoyed reading the genres: mystery, action, and adventure stories. His desire to read books even grew more as he continued to advance in elementary school in the fifth and sixth grades. People at the local public library knew him by name because he would walk ten miles to check out books and walk back home during the fifth and sixth grades even during the winter months. His love for books was channeled into high school when he became a Library Aide in high school at the local public library, a position that he held until he graduated from high school. The Librarian (Darlene DeHudy) enjoyed having DeVere work in the community. He wound up going to graduate school and earning a master's degree in Library and Information Science from the

University of Michigan along with obtaining a Bachelor of Science Degree in Education and another master's in Educational Technology. When he started his educational journey, he wanted to become a teacher but for some strange reason, his career landed on the runways of public libraries which eventually led him to become a media specialist working for over thirty years. The students just adored his dedication to libraries and public education. He was always a standout professional working in four different school districts. He was the first African American hired to work in a predominantly white district (Grand Haven Area Schools) in his state. The background and experience that he developed working in libraries were simply outstanding and extraordinary, shelving thousands of library books, ordering thousands of library books, checking out thousands of books, and working with just about every age group throughout his career in the library profession. Writing has been something that he had placed on the back burner for years until the development of his first manuscript that he had written during the Coronavirus Pandemic. He brings a tremendous amount of talent to the literary field based on this completed book that he is hoping that everyone reading it will enjoy it just as much as he did to create it. He has always been a Midwesterner.

CPSIA information can be obtained
at www.ICGtesting.com
Printed in the USA
JSHW011007120423
40210JS00001B/36

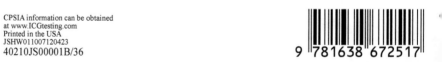

9 781638 672517